The Diabetic Kitchen

1500 Days of Nourishing and Flavorful Recipes with 4-Week Meal Plans to Lead A Healthy Lifestyle / Full Color Edition

Karly T. Whittington

Editor: AALIYAH LYONS

Interior Design: BROOKE WHITE

Cover Art: DANIELLE REES

Food stylist: SIENNA ADAMS

Table Of Contents

Introduction

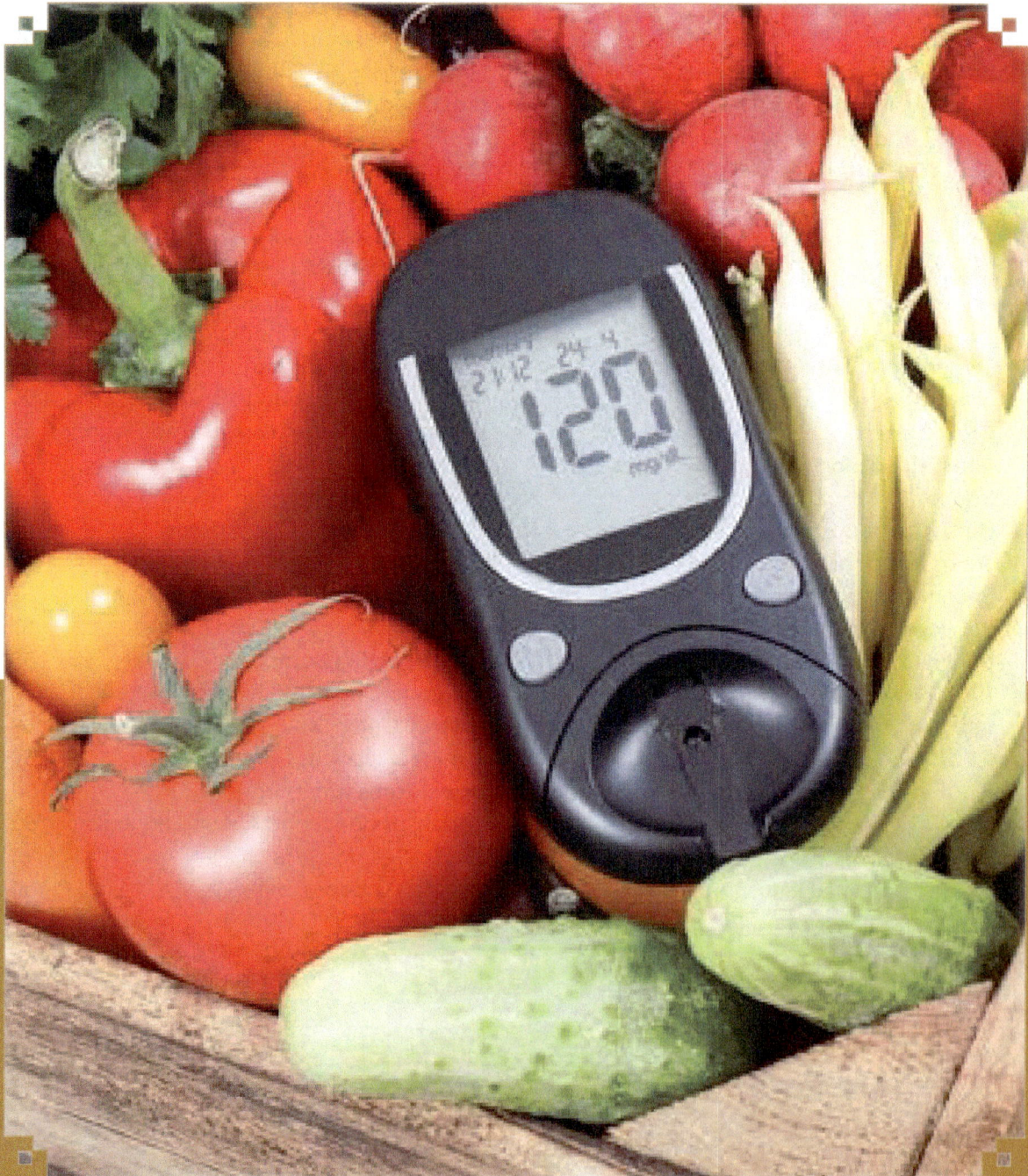

Step into "The Diabetic Kitchen," a culinary sanctuary where every dish is a delightful fusion of flavor, health, and creativity. In these pages, you'll embark on a delicious journey through a world of vibrant ingredients, tantalizing aromas, and mouthwatering recipes designed to support your diabetic lifestyle.

Living with diabetes doesn't mean sacrificing the pleasure of good food; it means embracing a new way of cooking and eating that nourishes both body and soul. As a chef passionate about promoting wellness through food, I've crafted this cookbook with one goal in mind: to empower you to take control of your health and indulge in the joys of cooking without compromise.

In "The Diabetic Kitchen," you'll discover a treasure trove of recipes that are as delicious as they are nutritious. From hearty breakfasts to satisfying mains and delectable desserts, each dish has been carefully crafted to strike the perfect balance between flavor, texture, and blood sugar management.

But this book is about more than just recipes; it's a celebration of the art of cooking and the joy of sharing meals with loved ones. It's about discovering new flavors, exploring fresh ingredients, and savoring every bite with gratitude and mindfulness.

Throughout these pages, you'll find practical tips and insights to help you navigate the grocery store with confidence, plan meals with ease, and make healthier choices every day. Whether you're cooking for yourself, your family, or hosting a gathering with friends, "The Diabetic Kitchen" is your trusted companion on the journey to better health through food.

So, join me in this culinary adventure as we explore the endless possibilities of the diabetic kitchen. Let's transform ordinary ingredients into extraordinary meals, and let every bite be a celebration of health, vitality, and pure deliciousness.

Here's to your health, happiness, and the joy of cooking!

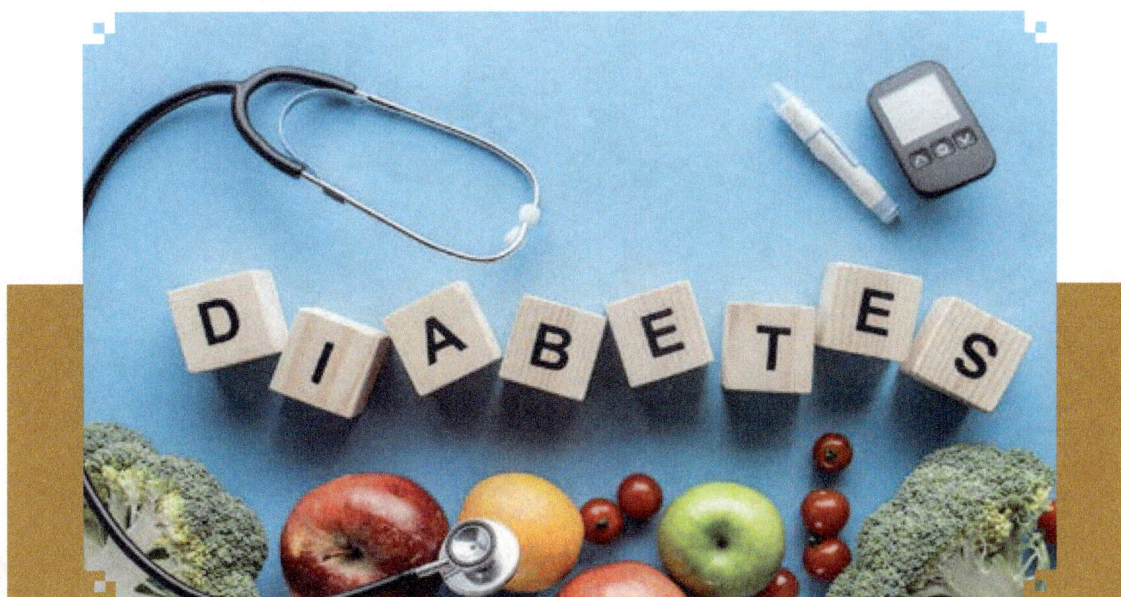

Chapter 1

Unlocking Diabetes

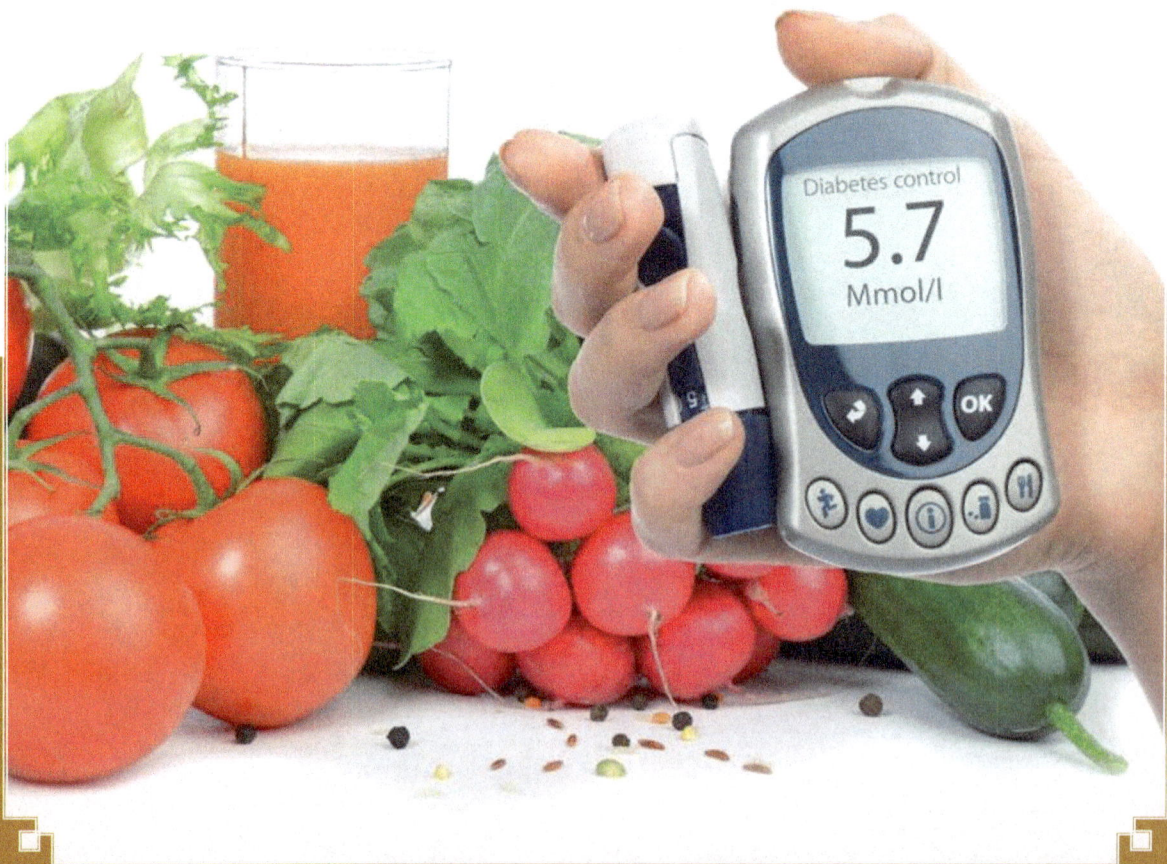

Understanding Diabetes and Nutrition

Living with diabetes necessitates a comprehensive understanding of how nutrition impacts one's health and well-being. This guide aims to demystify the relationship between diabetes and nutrition, offering clear and practical insights for individuals seeking to manage their condition effectively.

- What is Diabetes?

Diabetes is a chronic condition characterized by elevated blood sugar levels, resulting from either inadequate insulin production or the body's inability to effectively use insulin. There are primarily two types of diabetes: type 1 and type 2. Type 1 diabetes occurs when the body's immune system mistakenly attacks and destroys insulin-producing cells in the pancreas, while type 2 diabetes typically develops when the body becomes resistant to insulin or fails to produce enough insulin to maintain normal blood sugar levels.

THE ROLE OF NUTRITION IN DIABETES MANAGEMENT

Nutrition plays a pivotal role in diabetes management, as the foods we consume directly influence our blood sugar levels. By making informed dietary choices, individuals with diabetes can better regulate their blood sugar and reduce the risk of complications associated with the condition. Key principles of diabetes nutrition include:

- Carbohydrate Management: Carbohydrates have the most significant impact on blood sugar levels. Monitoring carbohydrate intake and choosing complex carbohydrates with a lower glycemic index can help stabilize blood sugar levels throughout the day.
- Balanced Meals: Consuming balanced meals that include a combination of carbohydrates, proteins, and fats can help prevent spikes in blood sugar. Pairing carbohydrates with lean proteins and healthy fats can slow the absorption of sugar into the bloodstream, promoting better blood sugar control.
- Portion Control: Controlling portion sizes is essential for managing blood sugar levels and maintaining a healthy weight. By measuring portions and avoiding oversized servings, individuals can prevent overeating and better manage their diabetes.
- Fiber-Rich Foods: Incorporating fiber-rich foods such as fruits, vegetables, whole grains, and legumes into the diet can improve blood sugar control and promote overall health. Fiber slows the absorption of sugar into the bloodstream and helps regulate digestion, reducing the risk of blood sugar spikes.
- Hydration: Staying hydrated is crucial for individuals with diabetes, as dehydration can exacerbate blood sugar fluctuations. Opting for water, herbal teas, and other low-calorie beverages can help maintain adequate hydration levels without adding excess sugar to the diet.

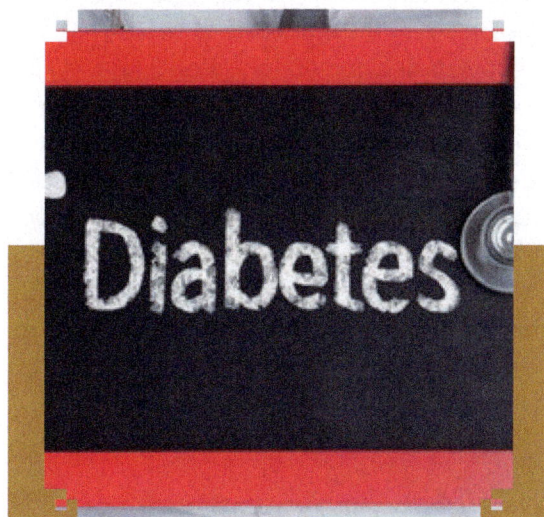

• The Types of Diabetes

Diabetes encompasses two primary types: type 1 and type 2. Type 1 diabetes typically develops in childhood or adolescence and results from the immune system mistakenly attacking and destroying insulin-producing cells in the pancreas. As a result, individuals with type 1 diabetes require lifelong insulin therapy to regulate their blood sugar levels.

In contrast, type 2 diabetes is more common and often develops later in life, although it can occur at any age. In type 2 diabetes, the body becomes resistant to insulin or fails to produce enough insulin to effectively regulate blood sugar levels. Lifestyle factors such as poor diet, sedentary behavior, and excess weight contribute to the development of type 2 diabetes, making it largely preventable through healthy lifestyle choices.

Additionally, there are other less common types of diabetes, including gestational diabetes, which occurs during pregnancy and usually resolves after childbirth. There are also forms of diabetes caused by specific genetic mutations, medications, or diseases affecting the pancreas.

Understanding the differences between these types of diabetes is essential for effective management and treatment. While type 1 diabetes requires insulin therapy, type 2 diabetes can often be managed through lifestyle modifications such as diet, exercise, and medication. Regardless of the type, proper management and regular monitoring are crucial for maintaining optimal health and preventing complications associated with diabetes.

Foods to Eat with Diabetes

NON-STARCHY VEGETABLES:

• Examples: Leafy greens (spinach, kale, lettuce), cruciferous vegetables (broccoli, cauliflower, Brussels sprouts), bell peppers, cucumbers, tomatoes, zucchini, mushrooms.
• Detailed Info: Non-starchy vegetables are low in carbohydrates and calories but high in fiber, vitamins, and minerals. They have a minimal impact on blood sugar levels, making them an excellent choice for individuals with diabetes. Aim to fill half your plate with non-starchy vegetables at each meal.

WHOLE GRAINS:

• Examples: Quinoa, brown rice, whole wheat bread, barley, oats, bulgur, buckwheat, whole grain pasta.
• Detailed Info: Whole grains are rich in fiber, which helps regulate blood sugar levels and promotes satiety. They also provide essential nutrients such as B vitamins, iron, and magnesium. Choose whole grains over refined grains to maximize nutritional benefits.

LEAN PROTEINS:

• Examples: Skinless poultry (chicken, turkey), fish (salmon, trout, tuna), lean cuts of beef or pork, tofu, tempeh, legumes (beans, lentils, chickpeas).
• Detailed Info: Lean proteins are essential for muscle repair, satiety, and blood sugar control. They provide important nutrients like iron, zinc, and omega-3 fatty acids without excess saturated fat or added sugars. Incorporate a variety of lean protein sources into your meals to meet your nutritional needs.

HEALTHY FATS:

• Examples: Avocado, nuts (almonds, walnuts, pistachios), seeds (chia seeds, flaxseeds, pumpkin seeds), olive oil, fatty fish (salmon, mackerel, sardines), nut butter (peanut butter, almond butter).

- Detailed Info: Healthy fats play a crucial role in heart health and overall well-being. They help stabilize blood sugar levels, reduce inflammation, and promote satiety. Choose sources of unsaturated fats, such as those found in plant-based foods and fatty fish, to support optimal health.

LOW-SUGAR FRUITS:

- Examples: Berries (strawberries, blueberries, raspberries), apples, citrus fruits (oranges, grapefruits, lemons), kiwi, cherries, peaches, plums.
- Detailed Info: Low-sugar fruits are rich in vitamins, minerals, and antioxidants while being lower in carbohydrates compared to high-sugar fruits like bananas and grapes. Enjoy these fruits in moderation as part of a balanced meal plan to satisfy your sweet cravings without causing significant spikes in blood sugar levels.

DAIRY AND DAIRY ALTERNATIVES:

- Examples: Greek yogurt, unsweetened almond milk, unsweetened soy milk, cottage cheese.
- Detailed Info: Dairy products provide essential nutrients like calcium, vitamin D, and protein. Opt for low-fat or non-fat dairy options to reduce saturated fat intake. Dairy alternatives like almond milk and soy milk can be suitable options for individuals who are lactose intolerant or prefer plant-based alternatives.

SNACKS:

- Examples: Raw vegetables with hummus, Greek yogurt with berries, a small handful of nuts, apple slices with almond butter, air-popped popcorn, hard-boiled eggs.
- Detailed Info: Healthy snacks can help

manage hunger between meals and prevent overeating. Choose snacks that combine protein, fiber, and healthy fats to keep you feeling satisfied and stabilize blood sugar levels. Pay attention to portion sizes and avoid high-calorie, high-sugar snacks.

Foods to Limit or Avoid

REFINED CARBS:

- Examples: White bread, white rice, sugary cereals, regular pasta, pastries, sugary snacks, sugary beverages (soda, fruit juice, sweetened tea).
- Detailed Info: Refined carbohydrates are quickly digested and can cause rapid spikes in blood sugar levels. They lack fiber and essential nutrients, contributing to poor blood sugar control and increased risk of weight gain, heart disease, and other health problems. Replace refined carbohydrates with whole grains to improve blood sugar management and overall health.

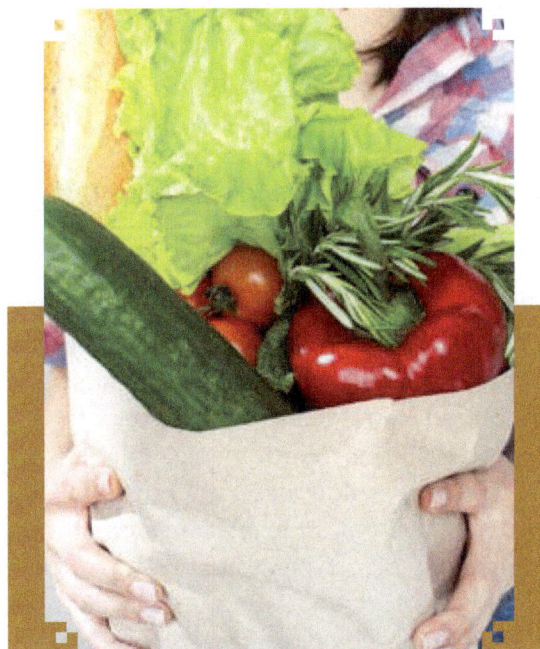

SUGARY FOODS AND BEVERAGES:

- Examples: Candy, cakes, cookies, ice cream, flavored yogurt, sugary cereals, sweetened coffee drinks, sweetened tea, fruit-flavored drinks, energy drinks.
- Detailed Info: Foods and beverages high in added sugars can cause dramatic fluctuations in blood sugar levels and contribute to insulin resistance over time. They provide empty calories and little to no nutritional value, increasing the risk of obesity, type 2 diabetes, and other chronic diseases. Choose low-sugar or sugar-free alternatives to satisfy your sweet cravings without compromising your health.

PROCESSED AND FRIED FOODS:

- Examples: Fast food (burgers, fries, fried chicken), processed meats (hot dogs, bacon, sausage), frozen meals, packaged snacks (chips, crackers, snack cakes), fried foods (fried chicken, French fries, onion rings).
- Detailed Info: Processed and fried foods are often high in unhealthy fats, sodium, and additives while lacking essential nutrients like fiber and vitamins. They can contribute to inflammation, insulin resistance, weight gain, and heart disease when consumed regularly. Opt for whole, unprocessed foods prepared using healthier cooking methods like baking, grilling, or steaming.

HIGH-SODIUM FOODS:

- Examples: Processed meats (bacon, sausage, deli meats), canned soups, canned vegetables, salty snacks (chips, pretzels), packaged meals, condiments (soy sauce, salad dressing, ketchup).
- Detailed Info: High-sodium foods can increase blood pressure and put strain on the heart and kidneys, especially for individuals with diabetes who are already at higher risk of heart disease and kidney problems. Limiting sodium intake can help prevent complications and promote overall health. Choose fresh or minimally processed foods and use herbs, spices, and lemon juice to flavor dishes instead of salt.

TRANS FATS AND SATURATED FATS:

- Examples: Margarine, shortening, processed snacks (crackers, cookies, pastries), fried foods, fatty cuts of meat, full-fat dairy products.
- Detailed Info: Trans fats and saturated fats can raise LDL (bad) cholesterol levels and increase the risk of heart disease, stroke, and insulin resistance. They are often found in processed and fried foods, as well as high-fat animal products. Opt for healthier fats like monounsaturated and polyunsaturated fats found in nuts, seeds, avocados, and fatty fish to protect heart health and improve insulin sensitivity.

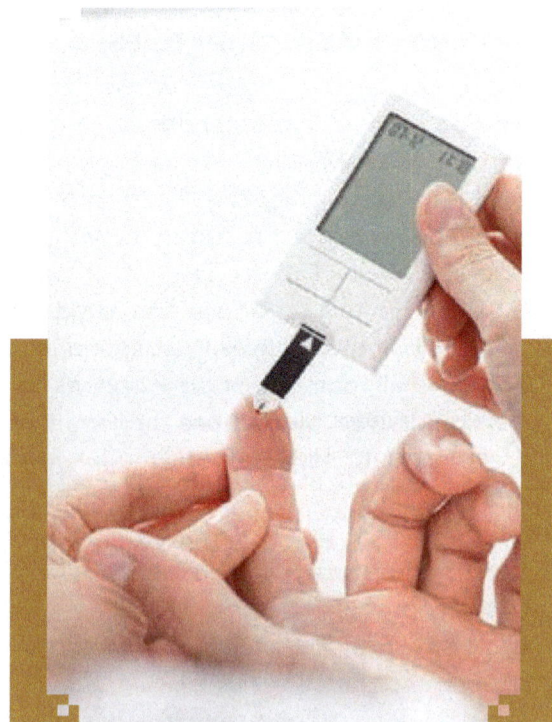

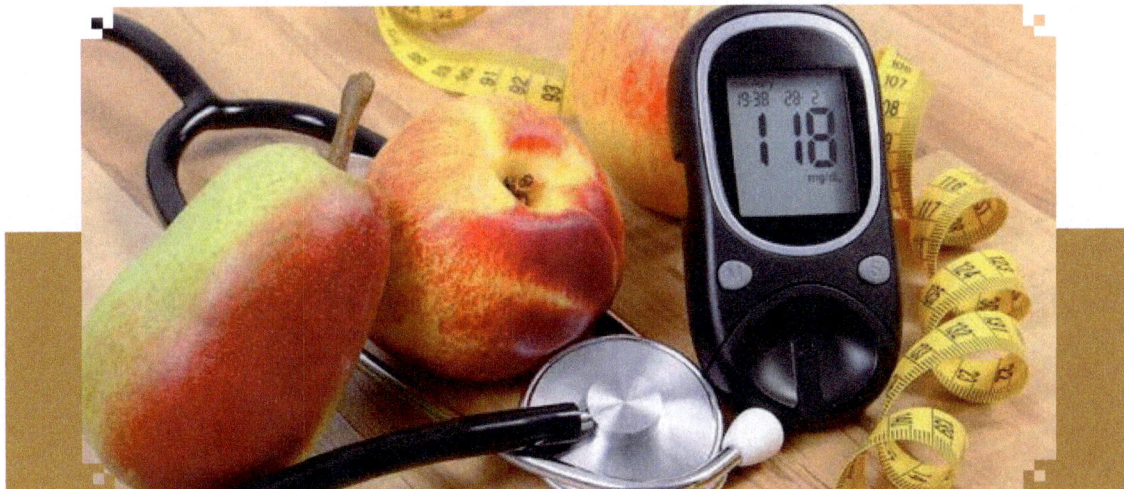

ALCOHOL:

- Examples: Beer, wine, spirits, mixed drinks, cocktails.
- Detailed Info: While moderate alcohol consumption may have some health benefits, excessive alcohol intake can interfere with blood sugar control and increase the risk of hypoglycemia (low blood sugar). Alcohol is also high in calories and can contribute to weight gain, especially when mixed with sugary mixers or consumed in large quantities. If you choose to drink alcohol, do so in moderation and monitor your blood sugar levels closely.

HIGH-GLYCEMIC INDEX FOODS:

- Examples: White bread, white rice, potatoes, sugary cereals, instant oatmeal, melons, pineapple, corn.
- Detailed Info: High-glycemic index foods are quickly digested and can cause rapid spikes in blood sugar levels, leading to fluctuations in energy levels and hunger. They can also contribute to insulin resistance over time and increase the risk of type 2 diabetes and heart disease.

Choose low-glycemic index alternatives like whole grains, legumes, non-starchy vegetables, and low-sugar fruits to help stabilize blood sugar levels and improve overall health.

In conclusion, embracing healthful eating habits is paramount for effectively managing diabetes and promoting overall well-being. By prioritizing whole, nutrient-rich foods, controlling portion sizes, and limiting added sugars and refined carbohydrates, individuals can better regulate blood sugar levels and reduce the risk of complications associated with diabetes. Additionally, incorporating sources of healthy fats, fiber-rich foods, and staying hydrated are essential components of a balanced diet for individuals with diabetes. Planning and preparing meals ahead of time can help foster consistency and adherence to healthful eating habits, while also minimizing reliance on processed or unhealthy options. Ultimately, by making conscious choices and prioritizing nutritious foods, individuals with diabetes can take control of their nutrition and improve their quality of life.

Chapter 2

4-Week Meal Plan

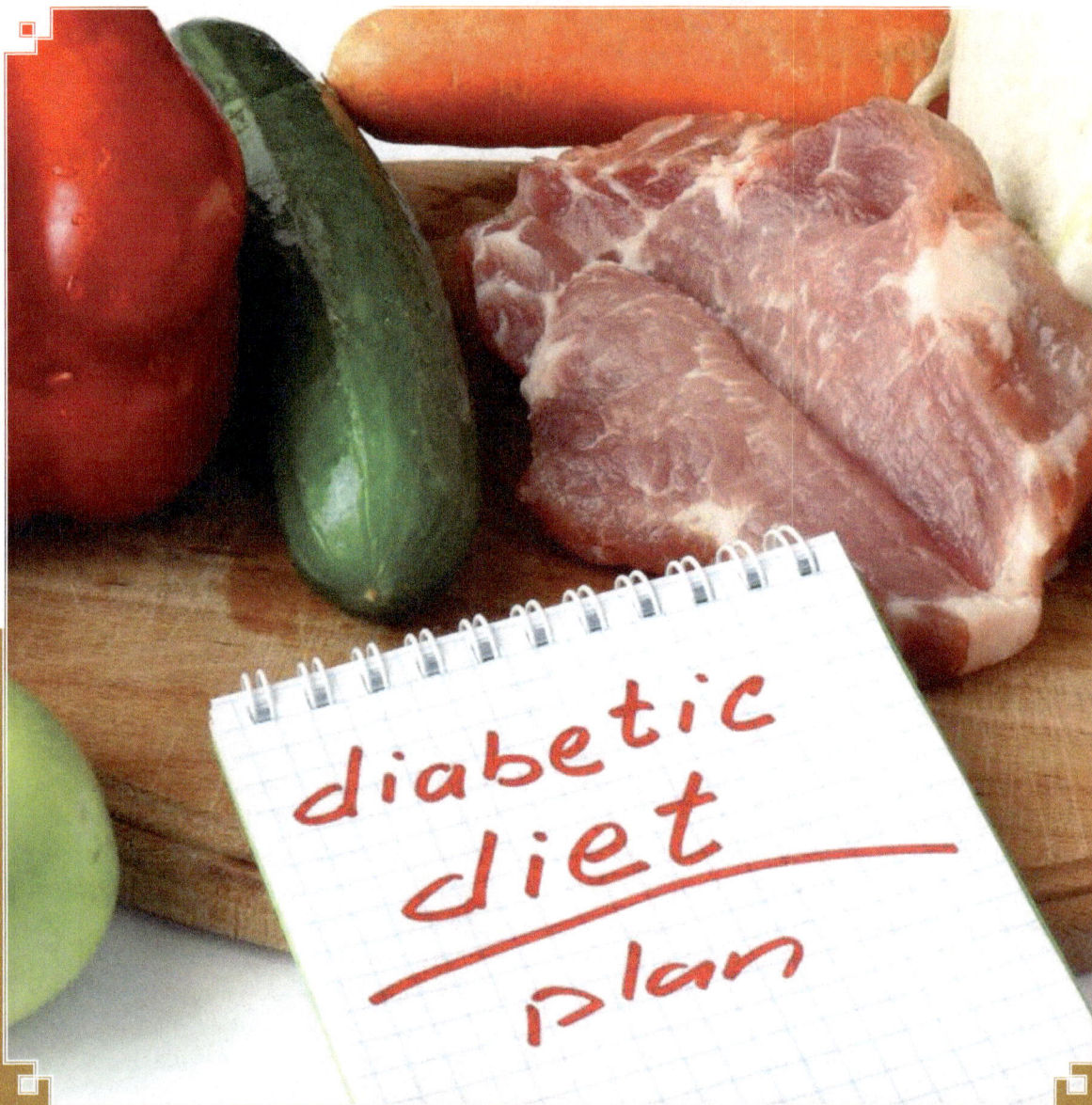

Week 1

DAY 1:
- Breakfast: Spanakopita Frittata
- Lunch: Teriyaki Turkey Meatballs
- Snack: Jewel Yams with Nutmeg
- Dinner: Sloppy Joes

Total for the day:
Calories: 756; Fat: 36.1 g; Protein: 68.1 g; Carbs: 54.9 g; Fiber: 12 g

DAY 2:
- Breakfast: Spanakopita Frittata
- Lunch: Teriyaki Turkey Meatballs
- Snack: Jewel Yams with Nutmeg
- Dinner: Sloppy Joes

Total for the day:
Calories: 756; Fat: 36.1 g; Protein: 68.1 g; Carbs: 54.9 g; Fiber: 12 g

DAY 3:
- Breakfast: Spanakopita Frittata
- Lunch: Teriyaki Turkey Meatballs
- Snack: Jewel Yams with Nutmeg
- Dinner: Sloppy Joes

Total for the day:
Calories: 756; Fat: 36.1 g; Protein: 68.1 g; Carbs: 54.9 g; Fiber: 12 g

DAY 4:
- Breakfast: Carrot Pear Smoothie
- Lunch: Sloppy Joes
- Snack: Jewel Yams with Nutmeg
- Dinner: Teriyaki Turkey Meatballs

Total for the day:
Calories: 684 ; Fat: 26 g; Protein: 59 g; Carbs: 70 g; Fiber: 15 g

DAY 5:
- Breakfast: Carrot Pear Smoothie

- Lunch: Teriyaki Turkey Meatballs
- Snack: Jewel Yams with Nutmeg
- Dinner: Teriyaki Turkey Meatballs

Total for the day:
Calories: 509; Fat: 25 g; Protein: 44 g; Carbs: 39 g;Fiber: 7 g

Week 2

DAY 1:
- Breakfast: Apple Filled Swedish Pancake
- Lunch: Mexican Turkey Tenderloin
- Snack: Carrot Cake Bites
- Dinner: Fennel and Chickpeas

Total for the day:
Calories: 644 ; Fat: 15 g; Protein: 48 g; Carbs: 70 g; Fiber: 20 g

DAY 2:
- Breakfast: Apple Filled Swedish Pancake
- Lunch: Mexican Turkey Tenderloin
- Snack: Carrot Cake Bites
- Dinner: Fennel and Chickpeas

Total for the day:
Calories: 644 ; Fat: 15 g; Protein: 48 g; Carbs: 70 g; Fiber: 20 g

DAY 3:
- Breakfast: Apple Filled Swedish Pancake
- Lunch: Mexican Turkey Tenderloin
- Snack: Carrot Cake Bites
- Dinner: Fennel and Chickpeas

Total for the day:
Calories: 644 ; Fat: 15 g; Protein: 48 g; Carbs: 70 g; Fiber: 20 g

DAY 4:
- Breakfast: Apple Filled Swedish Pancake
- Lunch: Fennel and Chickpeas
- Snack: Carrot Cake Bites

• Dinner: Mexican Turkey Tenderloin

Total for the day:
Calories: 644 ; Fat: 15 g; Protein: 48 g; Carbs: 70 g; Fiber: 20 g

DAY 5:
• Breakfast: Apple Filled Swedish Pancake
• Lunch: Fennel and Chickpeas
• Snack: Carrot Cake Bites
• Dinner: Mexican Turkey Tenderloin

Total for the day:
Calories: 644 ; Fat: 15 g; Protein: 48 g; Carbs: 70 g; Fiber: 20 g

Week 3

DAY 1:
• Breakfast: Breakfast Pizza
• Lunch: Cheesy Chicken and Spinach
• Snack: Oatmeal Cookies
• Dinner: Scallion Grits with Shrimp

Total for the day:
Calories: 865; Fat: 49 g; Protein: 69.2 g; Carbs: 37.1 g; Fiber: 2 g

DAY 2:
• Breakfast: Breakfast Pizza
• Lunch: Cheesy Chicken and Spinach
• Snack: Oatmeal Cookies
• Dinner: Scallion Grits with Shrimp

Total for the day:
Calories: 865; Fat: 49 g; Protein: 69.2 g; Carbs: 37.1 g; Fiber: 2 g

DAY 3:
• Breakfast: Breakfast Pizza
• Lunch: Cheesy Chicken and Spinach
• Snack: Oatmeal Cookies
• Dinner: Scallion Grits with Shrimp

Total for the day:
Calories: 865; Fat: 49 g; Protein: 69.2 g; Carbs: 37.1 g; Fiber: 2 g

DAY 4:
• Breakfast: Breakfast Pizza
• Lunch: Scallion Grits with Shrimp
• Snack: Oatmeal Cookies
• Dinner: Cheesy Chicken and Spinach

Total for the day:
Calories: 865; Fat: 49 g; Protein: 69.2 g; Carbs: 37.1 g; Fiber: 2 g

DAY 5:
• Breakfast: Breakfast Pizza
• Lunch: Scallion Grits with Shrimp
• Snack: Oatmeal Cookies
• Dinner: Cheesy Chicken and Spinach

Total for the day:
Calories: 865; Fat: 49 g; Protein: 69.2 g; Carbs: 37.1 g; Fiber: 2 g

Week 4

DAY 1:
• Breakfast: Breakfast Vegetable and Okra Hash
• Lunch: Coconut-Encrusted Chicken
• Snack: Fluffy Lemon Bars
• Dinner: Herb-Crusted Halibut

Total for the day:
Calories: 774; Fat: 31.1 g; Protein: 61.8 g; Carbs: 57.8 g;Fiber: 13.6 g

DAY 2:
• Breakfast: Breakfast Vegetable and Okra Hash
• Lunch: Coconut-Encrusted Chicken
• Snack: Fluffy Lemon Bars
• Dinner: Herb-Crusted Halibut

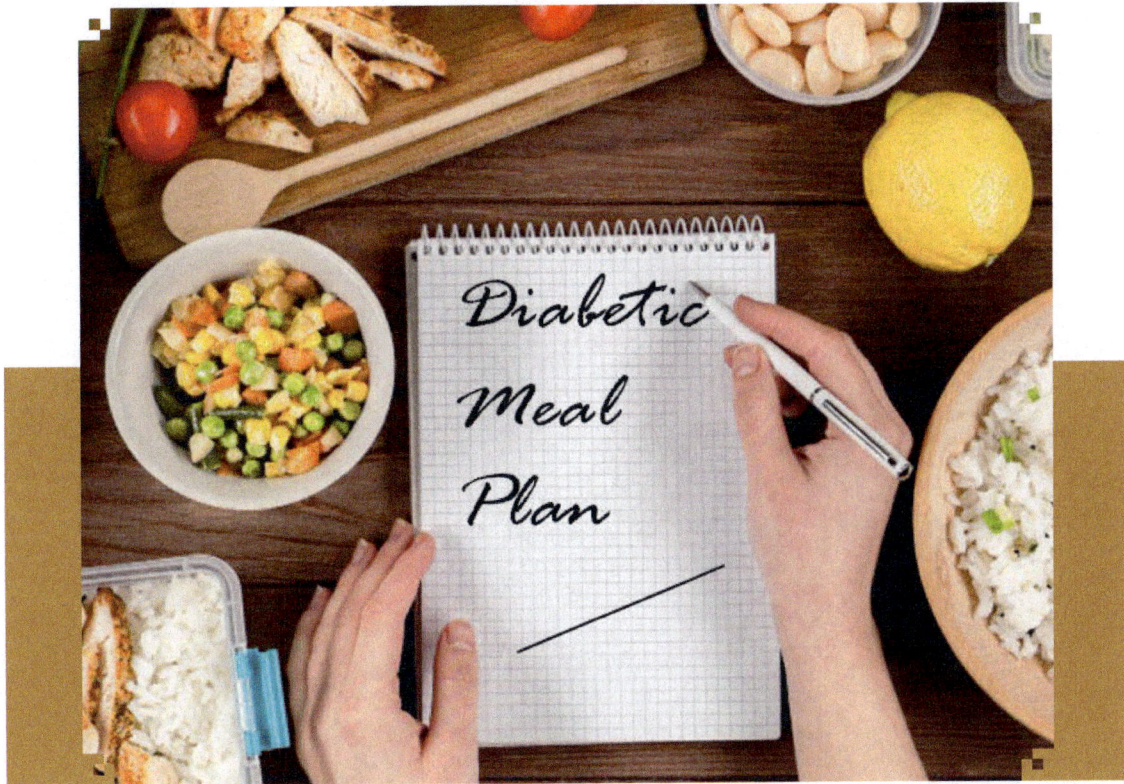

Total for the day:

Calories: 774; Fat: 31.1 g; Protein: 61.8 g; Carbs: 57.8 g;Fiber: 13.6 g

DAY 3:

- Breakfast: Breakfast Vegetable and Okra Hash
- Lunch: Coconut-Encrusted Chicken
- Snack: Fluffy Lemon Bars
- Dinner: Herb-Crusted Halibut

Total for the day:

Calories: 774; Fat: 31.1 g; Protein: 61.8 g; Carbs: 57.8 g;Fiber: 13.6 g

DAY 4:

- Breakfast: Breakfast Vegetable and Okra Hash

- Lunch: Herb-Crusted Halibut
- Snack: Fluffy Lemon Bars
- Dinner: Coconut-Encrusted Chicken

Total for the day:

Calories: 774; Fat: 31.1 g; Protein: 61.8 g; Carbs: 57.8 g;Fiber: 13.6 g

DAY 5:

- Breakfast: Breakfast Vegetable and Okra Hash
- Lunch: Coconut-Encrusted Chicken
- Snack: Fluffy Lemon Bars
- Dinner: Coconut-Encrusted Chicken

Total for the day:

Calories: 730; Fat: 33.9 g; Protein: 50.9 g; Carbs: 62.6 g; Fiber: 17.7 g

Chapter 3

Morning Pleasures

Sausage and Pepper Breakfast Burrito

Prep time: 10 minutes | Cook time: 15 minutes | Serves 4

- 8 ounces bulk pork breakfast sausage
- ½ onion, chopped
- 4 (6-inch) low-carb tortillas
- 1 cup shredded pepper jack cheese

1. In a large nonstick skillet on medium-high heat, cook the sausage, eggs and cook, stirring, until eggs are set, about 3 minutes more.
2. Serve with sour cream and salsa, if desired.

PER SERVING

Calories: 486 | Total Fat: 36g | Saturated Fat: 14g | Sodium: 810mg | Carbs: 13g | Fiber: 8g | Protein: 32g

Carrot Pear Smoothie

Prep time: 10 minutes | Cook time: 25 minutes | Serves 2

- 2 carrots, peeled and grated
- 1 ripe pear, unpeeled, cored and chopped
- 2 teaspoons grated fresh ginger
- juice and zest of 1 lime
- 1 cup water
- ½ teaspoon ground cinnamon
- ¼ teaspoon ground nutmeg

1. Put the carrots, pear, ginger, lime juice, lime zest, water, cinnamon, and nutmeg in a blender and blend until smooth.
2. Pour into two glasses and serve.

PER SERVING

Calories: 74 | Total Fat: 0g | Cholesterol: 0mg | Sodium: 43mg | Total Carbs: 19g | Sugar: 11g | Fiber: 4g | Protein: 1g

Apple Filled Swedish Pancake

Prep time: 25 minutes| Cook time: 20 minutes| Serves 6

- 2 apples, cored and sliced thin
- ¾ cup egg substitute
- ½ cup fat-free milk
- ½ cup sugar-free caramel sauce
- 1/8 tsp cloves
- 1/8 tsp salt
- Nonstick cooking spray

1. Heat oven to 400 degrees. Place margarine in cast iron, or ovenproof, skillet and place in oven until margarine is melted.
2. Pour the caramel sauce into a microwave-proof measuring glass and heat 30 – 45 seconds, or until warmed through.
3. To serve, spoon apples into pancake and drizzle with caramel. Cut into wedges.

PER SERVING

Calories: 193 |Total Carbs: 25g |Net Carbs: 23g |Protein: 6g |Fat: 2g |Sugar: 12g |Fiber: 2g

Spanakopita Frittata

Prep time: 10 minutes | Cook time: 15 minutes | Serves 4

- 2 tablespoons extra-virgin olive oil
- ½ sweet onion, chopped
- 1 red bell pepper, seeded and chopped
- ¼ teaspoon sea salt
- ½ teaspoon freshly ground black pepper
- 8 egg whites

1. Preheat the oven to 375°F (190°C).
2. Place a heavy ovenproof skillet over medium-high heat and add the olive oil.
3. Sauté the onion, bell pepper, and garlic until softened, about 5 minutes. Season with salt and pepper.
4. Loosen the edges of the frittata with a rubber spatula, then invert it onto a plate.
5. Garnish with the chopped parsley and serve.

PER SERVING

Calories: 146 | Fat: 10.1g | Protein: 10.1g | Carbs: 3.9g | Fiber: 1.0g | Sugar: 2.9g | Sodium: 292mg

Brussels Sprouts and Egg Scramble

Prep time: 5 minutes | Cook time: 20 minutes|
   Serves 4

- Avocado oil cooking spray
- 4 slices low-sodium turkey bacon
- 20 Brussels sprouts, halved lengthwise
- 8 large eggs
- ¼ cup crumbled feta, for garnish

1. Heat a large skillet over medium heat. When hot, coat the cooking surface with cooking spray and cook the bacon to your liking.
2. Place the Brussels sprouts in the skillet cut-side down, and cook for 3 minutes.
3. Crumble the bacon once it has cooled.
4. Divide the Brussels sprouts into 4 Add 1 tablespoon of feta to each portion.

PER SERVING

Calories: 253 | Total Fat: 15g | Protein: 21g | Carbs: 10g | Sugars: 4g | Fiber: 4g | Sodium: 343mg

Strawberry Coconut Scones

Prep time: 5 minutes| Cook time: 40 minutes|
   Serves 8

- 1 ½ cup strawberries, chopped
- 1 large egg
- 1 ½ cups almond flour
- ¼ cup coconut oil, melted
- 2 tbsp. cornstarch
- 1 tsp vanilla
- 1 tsp baking powder

1. Heat oven to 350 degrees. Line a 9-inch round baking dish with parchment paper.
2. In a large bowl, beat egg, oil, Splenda, and vanilla until smooth. Scrape sides as needed.
3. Let cool 15 minutes before removing from pan. Slice into 8 pieces.

PER SERVING

Calories: 225 |Total Carbs: 14g |Net Carbs: 11g |Protein: 5g |Fat: 17g |Sugar: 8g |Fiber: 3g

Cottage Pancakes

Prep time: 10 minutes | Cook time: 20 minutes | Serves 4

- 2 cups low-fat cottage cheese
- 4 egg whites
- 2 eggs
- 1 tablespoon pure vanilla extract
- 1½ cups almond flour
- Nonstick cooking spray

1. Place the cottage cheese, egg whites, eggs, and vanilla in a blender and pulse to combine.
2. Add the almond flour to the blender and blend until smooth.
3. Remove the pancakes to a plate and repeat with the remaining batter.
4. Serve with fresh fruit.

PER SERVING

Calories: 345 | Fat: 22.1g | Protein: 29.1g | Carbs: 11.1g | Fiber: 4.1g | Sugar: 5.1g | Sodium: 560mg

Golden Potato Cakes

Prep time: 10 minutes | Cook time: 25 minutes | Serves 4

- ½ pound russet potatoes, peeled, shredded, rinsed, and patted dry
- ¼ sweet onion, chopped
- sea salt
- freshly ground black pepper
- Nonstick cooking spray
- 1 cup unsweetened applesauce

1. Place the potatoes, onion, oil, and thyme in a large bowl and stir to mix well.
2. Place a large skillet over medium heat and lightly coat it with cooking spray.
3. Remove the cakes to a plate and repeat with the remaining mixture.
4. Serve with the applesauce.

PER SERVING

Calories: 106 | Total Fat: 3g | Cholesterol: 0mg | Sodium: 6mg | Total Carbs: 18g | Sugar: 7g | Fiber: 2g | Protein: 1g

Tropical Fruity Steel Cut Oats

Prep time: 5 minutes | Cook time: 20 minutes | Serves 4

- 1 cup steel cut oats
- 1 cup unsweetened almond milk
- 2 cups coconut water or water
- ¾ cup frozen chopped peaches
- ¾ cup frozen mango chunks

1. In the electric pressure cooker, combine the oats, almond milk, coconut water, peaches, mango chunks, and vanilla bean seeds and pod. Stir well.
2. Once the pin drops, unlock and remove the lid.
3. Discard the vanilla bean pod and stir well.
4. Spoon the oats into 4 bowls. Top each serving with a sprinkle of cinnamon and 1 tablespoon of the macadamia nuts.

PER SERVING

Calories: 126 | Fat: 7.1g | Protein: 1.9g | Carbs: 14.2g | Fiber: 2.9g | Sugar: 8.1g | Sodium: 166mg

Breakfast Vegetable and Okra Hash

Prep time: 15 minutes | Cook time: 30 minutes | Serves 6 t0 8

- 2 tablespoons extra-virgin olive oil
- 2 garlic cloves, minced
- 1 small yellow onion, finely chopped
- 4 russet potatoes, cut into 1-inch cubes
- 2 tablespoons Creole seasoning
- ¼ cup low-sodium broth
- 1 zucchini, roughly chopped
- 1 green bell pepper, roughly chopped
- 2 cups okra, cut into 1-inch rounds

1. Heat the olive oil in a skillet over medium-low heat.
2. Toss in the garlic and onion and sauté for 4 minutes, or until the onion is translucent.
3. Remove from the heat and serve on plates.

PER SERVING

Calories: 168 | Fat: 2.3g | Protein: 6.7g | Carbs: 30g | Fiber: 5.5g | Sugar: 3.7g | Sodium: 286mg

Caesar Chicken Sandwiches

Prep time: 5 minutes | Cook time: none | Serves 4

For The Dressing

- 4 tablespoons plain low-fat Greek yogurt
- 4 teaspoons Dijon mustard
- ⅛ teaspoon garlic powder

For The Sandwiches

- 2 cups shredded rotisserie chicken
- 1½ cups chopped romaine lettuce
- 12 cherry tomatoes, halved

To Make The Dressing

1. In a small bowl, whisk together the yogurt, mustard, lemon juice, Parmesan cheese, black pepper, and garlic powder.

To Make The Sandwiches

1. In a large bowl, combine the chicken, lettuce, and tomatoes. Divide the filling into four equal portions.

PER SERVING

Calories: 242 | Total Fat: 5g | Protein: 28g | Carbs: 25g | Sugars: 4g | Fiber: 8g | Sodium: 359mg

Egg Salad Sandwiches

Prep time: 10 minutes | Cook time: 0 minutes | Serves 4

- 8 large hardboiled eggs
- 3 tablespoons plain low-fat Greek yogurt
- 1 tablespoon mustard
- ½ teaspoon freshly ground black pepper
- 1 teaspoon chopped fresh chives
- 4 slices 100% whole-wheat bread
- 2 cups fresh spinach, loosely packed

1. Peel the eggs and cut them in half.
2. In a large bowl, mash the eggs with a fork, leaving chunks.
3. Add the yogurt, mustard, pepper, and chives, and mix.
4. For each portion, layer 1 slice of bread with one-quarter of the egg salad and spinach.

PER SERVING

Calories: 278 | Fat: 12.1g | Protein: 20.1g | Carbs: 23.1g | Fiber: 2.9g | Sugar: 3.1g | Sodium: 365mg

Chapter 4

Poultry Innovations

Saffron-Spiced Chicken Breasts

**Prep time: 10 minutes, plus 1 hour to marinate |
Cook time: 10 minutes | Serves 4**

- pinch saffron (3 or 4 threads)
- ½ cup plain nonfat yogurt
- 2 tablespoons water
- ½ onion, chopped
- 3 garlic cloves, minced
- 1 tablespoon extra-virgin olive oil

1. In a blender jar, combine the saffron, yogurt, water, onion, garlic, cilantro, lemon juice, and salt. Pulse to blend.
2. In a large skillet, heat the oil over medium heat. Add the chicken pieces, shaking off any excess marinade. flipping once, until cooked through and golden brown.

PER SERVING

Calories: 155 | Total Fat: 5g | Protein: 26g | Carbs: 3g | Sugars: 1g | Fiber: 0g | Sodium: 501mg

Mexican Turkey Tenderloin

**Prep time: 5 minutes | Cook time: 8 minutes |
Serves 6**

- 1 cup low-sodium Salsa or bottled salsa
- 1 teaspoon chili powder
- ½ teaspoon ground cumin
- ¼ teaspoon dried oregano
- Freshly ground black pepper
- ½ cup shredded Monterey Jack cheese or Mexican cheese blend

1. In a small bowl or measuring cup, combine the salsa, chili powder, cumin, and oregano. Pour half of the mixture into the electric pressure cooker.
2. Sprinkle the cheese on top, and put the lid back on for a few minutes to let the cheese melt.
3. Serve immediately.

PER SERVING

Calories: 168 | Total Fat: 5g | Protein: 28g | Carbs: 3g | Sugars: 2g | Fiber: 1g | Sodium: 559mg

Chicken with Balsamic Kale

**Prep time: 5 minutes | Cook time: 15 minutes |
Serves 4**

- 4 (4-ounce / 113-g) boneless, skinless chicken breasts
- ¼ teaspoon salt
- 1 tablespoon freshly ground black pepper
- 2 tablespoons unsalted butter
- 1 tablespoon extra-virgin olive oil
- ½ cup balsamic vinegar
- 20 cherry tomatoes, halved

1. Season both sides of the chicken breasts with the salt and pepper.
2. Add the vinegar and the tomatoes and cook for another 3 to 5 minutes.
3. Divide the kale and tomato mixture into four equal portions, and top each portion with 1 chicken breast.

PER SERVING

Calories: 294 | Fat: 11.1g | Protein: 31.1g | Carbs: 17.9g | Fiber: 3.1g | Sugar: 4.0g | Sodium: 330mg

Teriyaki Turkey Meatballs

**Prep time: 20 minutes | Cook time: 20 minutes |
Serves 6 (4 meatballs each)**

- 1 pound lean ground turkey
- ¼ cup finely chopped scallions, both white and green parts
- 1 egg
- 2 garlic cloves, minced
- 1 teaspoon grated fresh ginger
- 1 tablespoon honey
- 2 teaspoons mirin
- 1 teaspoon toasted sesame oil

1. Preheat the oven to 400°F. Line a baking sheet with parchment paper.
2. Bake for 10 minutes, flip with a spatula, and continue baking for an additional 10 minutes until the meatballs are cooked through.

PER SERVING

Calories: 153 | Total Fat: 8g | Protein: 16g | Carbs: 5g | Sugars: 4g | Fiber: 0g | Sodium: 270mg

Margarita Chicken Dip

Prep time: 10 minutes| Cook time: 1 hour| Serves 12

- 2 ½ cup Monterrey jack cheese, grated
- 1 ½ cup chicken, cooked and shredded
- ¼ cup fresh lime juice
- 2 tbsp. fresh orange juice
- 1 tsp cumin
- 1 tsp salt

1. Place the cream cheese on bottom of crock pot. Top with chicken, then grated cheese. Add remaining Ingredients, except the Pico de Gallo.
2. Cover and cook on low 60 minutes. Stir the dip occasionally to combine Ingredients.
3. When dip is done transfer to serving bowl. Top with Pico de Gallo and serve with tortilla chips.

PER SERVING

Calories: 169 |Total Carbs: 5g |Protein: 14g |Fat: 8g |Sugar: 1g |Fiber: 0g

Indian Flavor Milky Curry Chicken

Prep time: 15 minutes | Cook time: 35 minutes | Serves 4

- 2 teaspoons olive oil
- 1 tablespoon garlic, minced
- 2 tablespoons curry powder
- 1 tablespoon fresh ginger, grated
- 1 cup coconut milk
- 2 cups low-sodium chicken broth
- 1 carrot, peeled and diced
- 2 tablespoons fresh cilantro, chopped

1. Heat the olive oil in a saucepan over medium-high heat until shimmering.
2. Turn down the heat to low, then simmer for 20 minutes until tender. Stir periodically.
3. Pour them in a large bowl and spread the cilantro on top before serving.

PER SERVING

Calories: 328 | Fat: 16.9g | Protein: 29.1g | Carbs: 14.8g | Fiber: 1.1g | Sugar: 3.9g | Sodium: 274mg

Thai-Style Chicken Roll-Ups

Prep time: 15 minutes | Cook time: 15 minutes | Serves 4

- 1½ cups shredded cooked chicken breast
- 1 cup bean sprouts
- 1 cup shredded green cabbage
- ½ cup shredded carrots
- 1 garlic clove, minced
- ¼ teaspoon salt
- 4 (8-inch) low-carb whole-wheat tortillas

1. In a large mixing bowl, toss the chicken breast, bean sprouts, cabbage, carrots, scallions, and cilantro.
2. Fold in two opposite sides of the tortilla and roll up. Serve.

PER SERVING

Calories: 210 | Total Fat: 8g | Protein: 21g | Carbs: 17g | Sugars: 3g | Fiber: 10g | Sodium: 360mg

Cheesy Chicken and Spinach

Prep time: 10 minutes | Cook time: 45 minutes | Serves 6

- 3 chicken breasts, boneless, skinless and halved lengthwise
- 6 ounces (170 g) low fat cream cheese, soft
- 1 cup Mozzarella cheese, grated
- 2 tablespoons olive oil, divided
- 3 cloves garlic, diced fine
- 1 teaspoon Italian seasoning
- Nonstick cooking spray

1. Heat oven to 350°F (180°C). Spray a glass baking dish with cooking spray.
2. Bake for 35 to 40 minutes, or until chicken is cooked through. Serve.

PER SERVING

Calories: 362 | Fat: 25.0g | Protein: 31.2g | Carbs: 3.1g | Fiber: 0g | Sugar: 0g | Sodium: 376mg

Cheesy Stuffed Chicken Breasts

Prep time: 15 minutes, plus 15 minutes to chill | Cook time: 30 minutes | Serves 4

- 1 cup chopped roasted red pepper
- 2 ounces goat cheese
- 4 kalamata olives, pitted, finely chopped
- 1 tablespoon chopped fresh basil
- 1 tablespoon extra-virgin olive oil

1. Preheat the oven to 400°F.
2. In a small bowl, stir together the red pepper, goat cheese, olives, and basil until well mixed.
3. Place the filling in the refrigerator for about 15 minutes to firm it up.
4. Let the chicken breasts rest for 10 minutes, remove the toothpicks, and serve.

PER SERVING

Calories: 245 | Total Fat: 9g | Cholesterol: 88mg | Sodium: 279mg | Total Carbs: 3g | Sugar: 2g | Fiber: 1g | Protein: 35g

Lemon Pepper Wings

Prep time: 25 minutes | Cook time: 35 minutes | Serves 4

- 2 tablespoons grated lemon zest
- 1 tablespoon freshly ground black pepper
- 2 pounds of free-range chicken wings
- 1 teaspoon sea salt

1. Preheat the oven to 375 degrees ° F.
2. Pat the chicken with a paper towel.
3. Bake in preheated oven for 30 to 35 minutes, flipping halfway when chicken is pierced and juices are translucent.
4. Meanwhile, in a large bowl, combine the lemon juice, pepper, lemon zest and salt.
5. Add the wings to the lemon juice.
6. Coat evenly in juices.
7. Serve hot and enjoy!

PER SERVING

Calories: 286 | Total Carbs: 2.2g | Net Carbs: 1.8g | Protein: 27g | Fat: 15g | Sugar: 2.8g | Fiber: 1g

Chapter 5

Pork, Lamb & Beef Gourmet

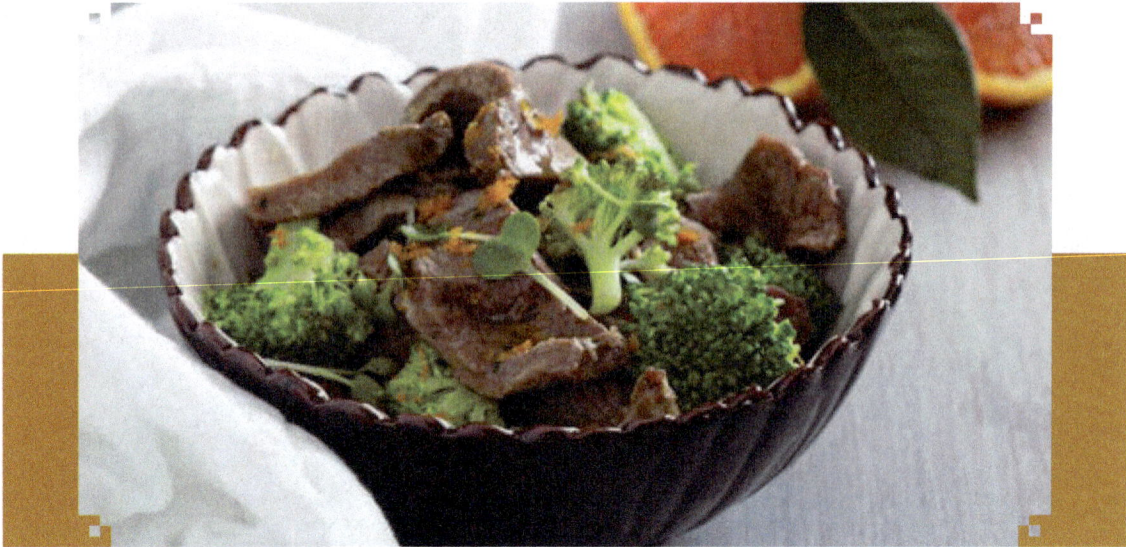

Rosemary Lamb Chops

Prep time: 25 minutes | Cook time: 2 minutes | Serves 4

- 1½ pounds lamb chops (4 small chops)
- 1 teaspoon kosher salt
- Leaves from 1 (6-inch) rosemary sprig
- 2 tablespoons avocado oil
- 1 tablespoon tomato paste
- 1 cup beef broth

1. Place the lamb chops on a cutting board. Press the salt and rosemary leaves into both sides of the chops. Let rest at room temperature for 15 to 30 minutes.
2. Set the electric pressure cooker to Sauté/More setting. When hot, add the avocado oil.
3. Place the lamb chops on plates and serve immediately.

PER SERVING

Calories: 233 | Total Fat: 18g | Protein: 15g | Carbs: 1g | Sugars: 1 | Fiber: 0g | Sodium: 450mg

Sofrito Beef Tips

Prep time: 5 minutes | Cook time: 30 minutes | Serves 6

- 1½ pounds stew beef chunks
- ½ head cauliflower
- 2 cups fresh or frozen broccoli florets
- 6 ounces recaíto cooking base

1. In a pressure cooker, place the beef on one side and the vegetables on the other. Pour in the recaíto.
2. Cook on the "Meat/Stew" setting.
3. When done cooking, mash the vegetables with a fork, breaking them down into a rice-like texture.
4. Divide the vegetables into six portions, and top each portion with one-sixth of the beef and sauce.

PER SERVING

Calories: 337 | Total Fat: 18g | Protein: 32g | Carbs: 6g | Sugars: 2; Fiber: 3g | Sodium: 294mg

Roasted Pork Loin with Carrots

Prep time: 5 minutes | Cook time: 40 minutes | Serves 4

- 1 pound (454 g) pork loin
- 1 tablespoon extra-virgin olive oil, divided
- 2 teaspoons honey
- ¼ teaspoon freshly ground black pepper
- ½ teaspoon dried rosemary

1. Preheat the oven to 350°F (180°C).
2. Rub the pork loin with ½ tablespoon of oil and the honey. Season with the pepper and rosemary.
3. Remove the baking sheet from the oven and let the pork rest for at least 10 minutes before slicing. Divide the pork and carrots into four equal portions.

PER SERVING

Calories: 344 | Fat: 10.1g | Protein: 26.1g | Carbs: 25.9g | Fiber: 3.9g | Sugar: 6.0g | Sodium: 110mg

Sirloin Korma

Prep time: 10 minutes | Cook time: 17–20 minutes | Serves 4

- 1 pound sirloin steak, sliced
- ½ cup plain yogurt
- 1 tablespoon curry powder
- 1 tablespoon olive oil
- 1 onion, chopped
- 2 garlic cloves, minced
- 1 tomato, diced
- ½ cup frozen baby peas, thawed

1. In a suitable bowl, combine the steak, yogurt, and curry powder.
2. Stir and set aside.
3. Stir in the peas and bake for almost 2 to 3 minutes or until hot.

PER SERVING

Calories: 299 | Fats: 11g | Net Carbs: 1g | Proteins: 38g | Total Carbs: 9g | Fiber: 2g | Sugars: 3g

Lamb, Mushroom, and Goat Cheese Burgers

Prep time: 15 minutes | Cook time: 15 minutes | Serves 4

- 8 ounces grass-fed ground lamb
- 8 ounces brown mushrooms, finely chopped
- ¼ teaspoon salt
- ¼ teaspoon freshly ground black pepper
- ¼ cup crumbled goat cheese
- 1 tablespoon minced fresh basil

1. In a large mixing bowl, combine the lamb, mushrooms, salt, and pepper, and mix well.
2. In a small bowl, mix the goat cheese and basil.
3. Heat the barbecue or a large skillet over medium-high heat. Add the burgers and cook for 5 to 7 minutes on each side, until cooked through. Serve.

PER SERVING

Calories: 173 | Total Fat: 13g | Protein: 11g | Carbs: 3g | Sugars: 1g | Fiber: 0g | Sodium: 154mg

Chipotle Chili Pork Chops

Prep time: 5 minutes, plus 4 hours to marinate | Cook time: 20 minutes | Serves 4

- juice and zest of 1 lime
- 1 tablespoon extra-virgin olive oil
- 1 tablespoon chipotle chili powder
- 1 teaspoon ground cinnamon
- pinch sea salt
- 4 (5-ounce) pork chops, about 1 inch thick
- lime wedges, for garnish

1. Combine the lime juice and zest, oil, chipotle chili powder, garlic, cinnamon, and salt in a resealable plastic bag. Add the pork chops. Remove as much air as possible and seal the bag.
2. Roast the chops until cooked through, turning once, about 10 minutes per side.
3. Serve with lime wedges.

PER SERVING

Calories: 204 | Total Fat: 9g | Cholesterol: 67mg | Sodium: 317mg | Total Carbs: 1g | Sugar: 1g | Fiber: 0g | Protein: 30g

Steak and Broccoli Bowls

Prep time: 10 minutes | Cook time: 15 minutes | Serves 4

- 2 tablespoons extra-virgin olive oil
- 2 cups broccoli florets
- 1 garlic clove, minced
- ½ teaspoon Chinese hot mustard
- Pinch red pepper flakes

1. In a large skillet over medium-high heat, heat the olive oil until it shimmers. with a slotted spoon, remove the beef from the oil and set it aside on a plate.
2. In a small bowl, whisk together the soy sauce, broth, mustard, and red pepper flakes.
3. Add the soy sauce mixture to the skillet and cook, stirring, until everything warms through, about 3 minutes.

PER SERVING

Calories: 230 | Fat: 11.1g | Protein: 27.1g | Carbs: 4.9g | Fiber: 1.0g | Sugar: 3.0g | Sodium: 376mg

Sloppy Joes

Prep time: 10 minutes | Cook time: 15 minutes | Serves 4

- 1 pound 93% lean ground beef
- ½ medium yellow onion, chopped
- 1 medium red bell pepper, chopped
- 4 sandwich thins, 100% whole-wheat
- 1 cup shredded cabbage

1. Heat a large skillet over medium heat. When hot, cook the beef, onion, and bell pepper for 7 to 10 minutes, stirring and breaking apart as needed.
2. Cut the sandwich thins in half so there is a top and a bottom. For each serving, place one-quarter of the filling and cabbage on the bottom half, then cover with the top half.

PER SERVING

Calories: 328 | Total Fat: 9g | Protein: 31g | Carbs: 36g | Sugars: 11g | Fiber: 8g | Sodium: 274mg

Beef and Pepper Fajita Bowls

Prep time: 10 minutes | Cook time: 15 minutes | Serves 4

- 4 tablespoons extra-virgin olive oil, divided
- 1 head cauliflower, riced
- 1 red bell pepper, seeded and sliced
- 2 garlic cloves, minced
- juice of 2 limes
- 1 teaspoon chili powder

1. In a large skillet over medium-high Add the cauliflower. Cook, stirring occasionally, until it softens, about 3 minutes. Set aside.
2. Return the beef along with any juices that have collected and the cauliflower to the pan. Cook, stirring, until everything is warmed through, 2 to 3 minutes.

PER SERVING

Calories: 310 | Total Fat: 18g | Saturated Fat: 3g | Sodium: 93mg | Carbs: 13g | Fiber: 3g | Protein: 27g

Mini Beef Meatloaf

Prep time: 15 minutes | Cook time: 25 minutes | Serves 6

- 1-lb. 80/20 ground beef
- ¼ yellow onion, peeled and chopped
- 1 large egg
- 2 tablespoons tomato paste
- ¼ cup water
- 1 tablespoon powdered erythritol

1. In a suitable bowl, combine ground beef, onion, pepper, egg, and almond flour.
2. Stir in the Worcestershire sauce, garlic powder and parsley to the bowl.
3. Mix until fully combined.
4. Adjust the temperature to 350 °F and set the timer for almost 25 minutes or until the internal temperature is 180 °F.
5. Serve warm.

PER SERVING

Calories: 170 | Fats: 9g | Net Carbs: 1g | Proteins: 15g | Total Carbs: 3g | Fat:s: 9g | Fiber: 1g | Sugars: 2g sodium: 85mg

Lamb Lettuce Cups with Garlic Yogurt

Prep time: 8 minutes | Cook time: 14 minutes | Serves 4

- 1 lb. ground lamb
- 1 tbsp. garlic, chopped and divided
- ½ tbsp. oregano, finely chopped
- 1 lemon, juiced and divided
- 8 crisp lettuce leaves
- 2 cups romaine lettuce, shredded
- ½ cup ricotta cheese, crumbled

1. Mix the ground lamb, ½ tablespoons chopped garlic, chopped oreganoand ground black pepper in a large mixing basin.
2. In a heavy bottomed pan, heat the remaining olive oil until it is hot.
3. Turn off the heat.

PER SERVING

Calories: 463 | Total Fat: 35g | Protein: 31g | Total Carbs: 6g | Net Carbs: 5g

Cajun Beef and Rice Skillet

Prep time: 10 minutes | Cook time: 25 minutes | Serves 4

- ¾ pound (340 g) lean ground beef
- 2 cup cauliflower rice, cooked
- 1 red bell pepper, sliced thin
- ½ yellow onion, diced
- ¼ cup fresh parsley, diced
- ½ cup low sodium beef broth
- 4 teaspoons Cajun seasoning

1. Place beef and 1½ teaspoons Cajun seasoning in a large skillet over medium-high heat. Cook, breaking apart with wooden spoon, until no longer pink, about 10 minutes.
2. Add broth and stir, scraping brown bits from the bottom of the pan. Remove from heat, stir in parsley and serve.

PER SERVING

Calories: 200 | Fat: 6.0g | Protein: 28.1g | Carbs: 8.1g | Fiber: 2.0g | Sugar: 4.0g | Sodium: 291mg

Chapter 6

Fish & Seafood Bonanza

Lemon Butter Cod with Asparagus

Prep time: 5 minutes | Cook time: 15 minutes | Serves 4

- ½ cup uncooked brown rice or quinoa
- 4 (4-ounce) cod fillets
- ¼ teaspoon salt
- ¼ teaspoon freshly ground black pepper
- 1 tablespoon freshly squeezed lemon juice

1. Cook the rice according to the package instructions.
2. Meanwhile, season both sides of the cod fillets with the salt, pepper, and garlic powder.
3. Cover and cook for 8 minutes.
4. Divide the rice, fish, and asparagus into four equal portions. Drizzle with the lemon juice to finish.

PER SERVING

Calories: 230 | Total Fat: 8g | Protein: 22g | Carbs: 20g | Sugars: 2g | Fiber: 5g | Sodium: 274mg

Tartar Tuna Patties

Prep time: 5 minutes | Cook time: 8 to 10 minutes | Serves 4

- 1 pound (454 g) canned tuna, drained
- 1 cup whole-wheat bread crumbs
- 2 large eggs, lightly beaten
- Juice and zest of 1 lemon
- ½ onion, grated
- 1 tablespoon chopped fresh dill
- 3 tablespoons extra-virgin olive oil
- ½ cup tartar sauce, for topping

1. Mix together the tuna with the bread crumbs, beaten eggs, lemon juice and zest, onion, and dill in a large bowl, and stir until well incorporated.
2. Remove the patties from the heat and top with the tartar sauce.

PER SERVING

Calories: 529 | Fat: 33.6g | Protein: 34.9g | Carbs: 18.3g | Fiber: 2.1g | Sugar: 3.8g | Sodium: 673mg

Lemon Trout with Garlic Potato Hash Browns

Prep time: 10 minutes | Cook time: 20 minutes | Serves 4

- 2 large russet potatoes, chopped
- ¼ onion, chopped
- 2 teaspoons minced garlic
- ½ teaspoon smoked paprika
- 2 tablespoons olive oil, divided
- 1 lemon, quartered

1. Preheat the oven to 400°F. Line a baking sheet with parchment paper.
2. Bake for about 20 minutes, tossing halfway through, until the potatoes are golden and lightly crispy and the fish is flaky.
3. Serve topped with parsley and lemon wedges.

PER SERVING:

Calories: 349 | Total fat: 10g | Saturated fat: 2g | Sodium: 85mg | Carbs: 35g | Sugar: 2g | Fiber: 3g | Protein: 27g

Crab Cakes

Prep time: 10 minutes| Cook time: 10 minutes| Serves 8

- 1 lb. lump blue crabmeat
- ¼ cup Dijon mustard
- 2 tbsp. sunflower oil
- 1 tbsp. baking powder
- 1 tbsp. Worcestershire sauce
- 1 ½ tsp old bay

1. In a small bowl, whisk together ¼ cup mayonnaise, Dijon mustard, Worcestershire, and lemon juice until combined. Cover and chill until ready to serve.
2. Cook 2 minutes or until firm, then flip and cook another minute. Transfer to serving plate. Serve with mustard dipping sauce.

PER SERVING

Calories: 96 |Total Carbs: 3g |Protein: 12g |Fat: 4g |Sugar: 1g |Fiber: 0g

Roasted Salmon with Honey-Mustard Sauce

Prep time: 5 minutes | Cook time: 20 minutes | Serves 4

- Nonstick cooking spray
- 2 tablespoons whole-grain mustard
- 1 tablespoon honey
- 2 garlic cloves, minced
- ¼ teaspoon salt
- ¼ teaspoon freshly ground black pepper
- 1 pound salmon fillet

1. Preheat the oven to 425°F. Spray a baking sheet with nonstick cooking spray.
2. In a small bowl, whisk together the mustard, honey, garlic, salt, and pepper.
3. Roast for 15 to 20 minutes, depending on the thickness of the fillet, until the flesh flakes easily.

PER SERVING

Calories: 186 | Total Fat: 7g | Protein: 23g | Carbs: 6g | Sugars: 4g | Fiber: 0g | Sodium: 312mg

Herb-Crusted Halibut

Prep time: 10 minutes | Cook time: 20 minutes | Serves 4

- 4 (5-ounce) halibut fillets
- extra-virgin olive oil, for brushing
- ½ cup coarsely ground unsalted pistachios
- 1 teaspoon chopped fresh thyme
- 1 teaspoon chopped fresh basil
- Pinch sea salt
- Pinch freshly ground black pepper

1. Preheat the oven to 350°F.
2. Line a baking sheet with parchment paper.
3. Pat the halibut fillets dry with a paper towel and place them on the baking sheet.
4. Serve immediately.

PER SERVING

Calories: 262 | Total Fat: 11g | Cholesterol: 45mg | Sodium: 77mg | Total Carbs: 4g | Sugar: 1g | Fiber: 2g | Protein: 32g

Tuna Carbonara

Prep time: 5 minutes| Cook time: 25 minutes|
Serves 4

- ½ lb. tuna fillet, cut in pieces
- 2 eggs
- 4 tbsp. fresh parsley, diced
- ½ recipe Homemade Pasta, cook & drain
- ½ cup reduced fat parmesan cheese
- 2 cloves garlic, peeled
- 2 tbsp. extra virgin olive oil
- Salt & pepper, to taste

1. In a small bowl, beat the eggs, parmesan and a dash of pepper.
2. Salt and pepper to taste and serve garnished with parsley.

PER SERVING

Calories: 409 |Total Carbs: 7g |Net Carbs: 6g |Protein: 25g |Fat: 30g |Sugar: 3g |Fiber: 1g

Sesame Salmon with Bok Choy

Prep time: 12 minutes | Cook time: 18 minutes |
Serves 4

- 4 (4-ounce) salmon fillets
- 4 teaspoons olive oil, divided
- ¼ cup maple syrup
- juice of 1 lemon

1. Preheat the oven to 400°F. Line a baking sheet with parchment paper and set aside.
2. Bake until the fish flakes easily with a fork and the bok choy is tender-crisp, about 15 minutes. Serve.

PER SERVING:

Calories: 329 | Total fat: 17g | Saturated fat: 3g | Sodium: 108mg | Carbs: 19g | Sugar: 12g | Fiber: 5g | Protein: 25g

Scallops Egg Salad

Prep time: 10 minutes | Cook time: 10 minutes | Serves 2

For Dressing
- 2 tablespoons plain Greek yogurt
- ½ teaspoon Dijon mustard
- Salt and black pepper, to taste

For Salad
- ¼ pound cooked scallops
- 1 hard-boiled egg, peeled and sliced

1. For the dressing: in a suitable bowl, add all the recipe ingredients and beat until well combined.
2. Drizzle with dressing and serve immediately.

PER SERVING

Calories: 183 | Fat: 5.4g | Total Carbs: 5.4g | Fiber: 0.4g | Sugar: 1.1g | Net Carbs: 2g | Protein: 26.1g

Panko Coconut Shrimp

Prep time: 12 minutes | Cook time: 6 to 8 minutes | Serves 4

- 2 egg whites
- 1 tablespoon water
- ½ cup whole-wheat panko bread crumbs
- ¼ cup unsweetened coconut flakes
- ½ teaspoon turmeric
- ½ teaspoon ground coriander

1. Preheat the air fry to 400°F (205°C).
2. In a shallow dish, beat the egg whites and water until slightly foamy. Set aside.
3. Air fry for 6 to 8 minutes, flipping the shrimp once during cooking, or until the shrimp are golden brown and cooked through.

PER SERVING

Calories: 181 | Fat: 4.2g | Protein: 27.8g | Carbs: 9.0g | Fiber: 2.3g | Sugar: 0.8g | Sodium: 227mg

Broiled Cod with Mango Salsa

Prep time: 10 minutes | Cook time: 5 to 10 minutes | Serves 4

Cod:
- 1 pound (454 g) cod, cut into 4 fillets, pin bones removed
- 2 tablespoons extra-virgin olive oil
- ¾ teaspoon sea salt, divided

Mango Salsa:
- 1 mango, pitted, peeled, and cut into cubes
- ¼ cup chopped cilantro
- Juice of 1 lime
- 1 garlic clove, minced

1. Preheat the broiler to high.
2. Place the cod fillets on a rimmed baking sheet. Brush both sides of the fillets with the olive oil. Sprinkle with ½ teaspoon of the salt.
3. Serve the cod warm topped with the mango salsa.

PER SERVING

Calories: 198 | Fat: 8.1g | Protein: 21.2g | Carbs: 13.2g | Fiber: 2.2g | saturated fat: 1g | Sodium: 355mg

Margarita Grilled Salmon

Prep time: 5 minutes| cook time 15 minutes| Serves 8

- 2-3 lb. salmon, with skin
- 2 limes, sliced thin
- 1 lime, juiced and zested
- 1 avocado
- 3 tbsp. lite mayonnaise
- 1 tsp olive oil
- 1 tsp tequila
- 1 tsp salt

1. In a small bowl, combine the lime zest, juice, tequila, olive oil and salt.
2. Spray the skin side of the fish with cooking spray. Lay on a large cookie sheet and cover with the marinade. Let sit for 30 minutes.
3. Place the avocado, mayonnaise and garlic in a blender or food processor and pulse until smooth and combined. Serve along with the fish.

PER SERVING

Calories: 413 |Total Carbs: 7g |Protein: 45g |Fat: 23g |Sugar: 1g |Fiber: 3g

Chapter 7

Delicious Vegetables and Salads

Stewed Chickpeas and Tomatoes

Prep time: 10 minutes | Cook time: 10 minutes | Serves 6

- 2 tablespoons avocado oil
- ½ cup finely chopped onion
- 1 cup Vegetable Broth, divided
- 2 garlic cloves, minced
- 1 tablespoon smoked paprika
- 1 tablespoon tomato paste
- 1 (15-ounce) can crushed tomatoes

1. Set the electric pressure cooker to the Sauté setting. When the pot is hot, pour in the avocado oil.
2. Stir in the kale and let everything sit in the pot for about 10 minutes or until the kale wilts.
3. Spoon into bowls and serve.

PER SERVING

Calories: 232 | Total Fat: 7g | Protein: 10g | Carbs: 35g | Sugars: 9g | Fiber: 10g | Sodium: 138mg

Stuffed Portobello Mushrooms

Prep time: 5 minutes | Cook time: 20 minutes | Serves 4

- 8 large portobello mushrooms
- 3 teaspoons extra-virgin olive oil, divided
- 4 cups fresh spinach
- 1 medium red bell pepper, diced
- ¼ cup crumbled feta

1. Preheat the oven to 450°F.
2. On a baking sheet, place the mushrooms cap-side down, and roast for 20 minutes.
3. Remove the mushrooms from the oven. Drain, if necessary. Spoon the spinach and pepper mix into the mushrooms, and top with feta.

PER SERVING

Calories: 116 | Total Fat: 6g | Protein: 7g | Carbs: 12g | Sugars: 6g | Fiber: 4g | Sodium: 126mg

Quinoa with Chopped Pistachios

Prep time: 10 minutes | Cook time: 20 minutes | Serves 4

- 1 tablespoon olive oil
- 1 onion, chopped
- 1 tablespoon minced garlic
- 1 teaspoon peeled and grated fresh ginger
- freshly ground black pepper
- ¼ cup chopped roasted pistachios
- 2 tablespoons chopped fresh parsley

1. In a large saucepan, heat the oil over medium-high heat and sauté the onion, garlic, and ginger for about 3 minutes, until softened.
2. Season with salt and pepper and serve topped with pistachios and parsley.

PER SERVING:

Calories: 245 | Total fat: 10g | Saturated fat: 1g | Sodium: 44mg | Carbs: 32g | Sugar: 2g | Fiber: 5g | Protein: 8g

Ginger Broccoli

Prep time: 10 minutes | Cook time: 10 minutes | Serves 4

- 1 tablespoon extra-virgin olive oil
- ½ sweet onion, thinly sliced
- 2 teaspoons grated fresh ginger
- 1 teaspoon minced fresh garlic
- 2 heads broccoli, cut into small florets
- ¼ cup low-sodium chicken broth
- sea salt
- freshly ground black pepper

1. Place a large skillet over medium-high heat and add the oil.
2. Sauté the onion, ginger, and garlic until softened, about 3 minutes.
3. Season with salt and pepper.
4. Serve immediately.

PER SERVING

Calories: 102 | Total Fat: 4g | Cholesterol: 0mg | Sodium: 109mg | Total Carbs: 14g | Sugar: 4g | Fiber: 5g | Protein: 5g

Summer Veggie Scramble

Prep time: 10 minutes | Cook time: 10 minutes | Serves 4

- 1 teaspoon extra-virgin olive oil
- ½ zucchini, diced
- 8 large eggs, beaten
- 1 tomato, cored, seeded, and diced
- 2 teaspoons chopped fresh oregano
- sea salt
- freshly ground black pepper

1. Place a large skillet over medium heat and add the olive oil..
2. Add the tomato and oregano to the skillet and stir to incorporate.
3. Serve seasoned with salt and pepper.

PER SERVING

Calories: 196 | Total Fat: 11g | Cholesterol: 432mg | Sodium: 156mg | Total Carbs: 4g | Sugar: 2g | Fiber: 1g | Protein: 13g

Roasted Cauliflower with Lime Juice

Prep time: 5 minutes | Cook time: 25 minutes | Serves 4

- 1 cauliflower head, broken into small florets
- 2 tablespoons extra-virgin olive oil
- ½ teaspoon salt, or more to taste
- ½ teaspoon ground chipotle chili powder
- Juice of 1 lime

1. Preheat the oven to 450°F (235°C) and line a large baking sheet with parchment paper. Set aside.
2. Remove from the oven and season as needed with salt.
3. Cool for 6 minutes and drizzle with the lime juice, then serve.

PER SERVING

Calories: 100 | Fat: 7.1g | Protein: 3.2g | Carbs: 8.1g | Fiber: 3.2g | Sugar: 3.2g | Sodium: 285mg

Pesto Stuffed Mushrooms

Prep time: 5 minutes| Cook time: 20 minutes| Serves 4

- 12 cremini mushrooms, stems removed
- 4 oz. low fat cream cheese, soft
- ½ cup mozzarella cheese, grated
- 1/3 cup reduced fat parmesan cheese
- 6 tbsp. basil pesto
- nonstick cooking spray

1. Heat oven to 375 degrees. Line a square baking dish with foil and spray with cooking spray. Arrange the mushrooms in the baking pan. Set aside.
2. Bake 20-23 minutes or until cheese is melted and golden brown. Let cook 5-10 minutes before serving.

PER SERVING

Calories: 76 |Total Carbs: 4g |Protein: 8g |Fat: 3g |Sugar: 1g |Fiber: 0g

Fennel and Chickpeas

Prep time: 10 minutes | Cook time: 20 minutes | Serves 6

- 1 tablespoon extra-virgin olive oil
- 1 small fennel bulb, trimmed and cut into ¼-inch-thick slices
- 1 cup low-sodium chicken broth
- 2 teaspoons chopped fresh thyme

1. Place a large saucepan over medium-high heat and add the oil.
2. Add the chickpeas, broth, thyme, salt, and pepper.
3. Remove the pan from the heat and stir in the butter.
4. Serve hot.

PER SERVING

Calories: 215 | Total Fat: 5g | Cholesterol: 5mg | Sodium: 253mg | Total Carbs: 32g | Sugar: 2g | Fiber: 15g | Protein: 12g

Broiled Plum Tomatoes with Goat Cheese

Prep time: 10 minutes | Cook time: 10 minutes | Serves 4

- 1 tablespoon olive oil
- 2 teaspoons minced garlic
- sea salt
- freshly ground black pepper
- ½ cup crumbled goat cheese
- 1 tablespoon chopped fresh oregano

1. Preheat the oven to broil.
2. Broil the tomatoes for about 6 minutes, until softened and lightly charred.
3. Sprinkle with the oregano and serve.

PER SERVING:

Calories: 92 | Total fat: 7g | Saturated fat: 3g | Sodium: 110mg | Carbs: 5g | Sugar: 3g | Fiber: 2g | Protein: 4g

Autumn-Inspired Fall Slaw

Prep time: 30 minutes | Cook time: 15 minutes | Serves 4

For the dressing
- ¼ cup extra-virgin olive oil
- 1 tablespoon maple syrup

For the salad
- ½ small butternut squash, shredded
- 1 tablespoon chopped fresh thyme

To make the dressing
1. In a small bowl, whisk together the oil, well blended. Set aside.

To make the salad
1. In a large bowl, toss the squash, red Add the dressing, toss, and serve.

PER SERVING:

Calories: 252 | Total fat: 17g | Saturated fat: 2g | Sugar: 17g | Fiber: 4g | Protein: 2g

Baked Egg Skillet with Avocado

Prep time: 5 minutes | Cook time: 25 minutes | Serves 4

- 2 tablespoons extra-virgin olive oil
- 1 red onion, chopped
- 1 green bell pepper, seeded and chopped
- 1 sweet potato, cut into ½-inch pieces
- 1 teaspoon chili powder
- ½ teaspoon sea salt
- 4 large eggs
- ½ cup shredded pepper jack cheese
- 1 avocado, cut into cubes

1. Preheat the oven to 350°F.
2. Bake until the eggs set, about 10 minutes.
3. Top with avocado before serving.

PER SERVING

Calories: 284 | Total Fat: 21g | Saturated Fat: 6g | Sodium: 264mg | Carbs: 16g | Fiber: 5g | Protein: 12g

Lettuce Salad with Olive Oil Dressing

Prep time: 10 minutes | Cook time: 0 minute | Serves 4

- 1 cup coarsely chopped iceberg lettuce
- 1 cup coarsely chopped romaine lettuce
- 1 cup baby spinach
- 1 cup diced cucumber
- 2 tablespoons olive oil
- ¼ teaspoon of sea salt

1. In a suitable bowl, combine the spinach and lettuces.
2. Add the tomato and cucumber.
3. Drizzle with oil and sprinkle with sea salt.
4. Mix well, then you can serve and enjoy.

PER SERVING

Calories: 159 | Total Carbs: 4 g | Net Carbs: 1.2g | Protein: 12 g | Fat: 12g | Sugars 0.5 g | Fiber: 6g

Chapter 8

Soup & Stew Extravaganza

Fast Split Pea Soup

Prep time: 8 minutes | Cook time: 15 minutes | Serves 4

- 1½ cups dried green split peas, rinsed and drained
- 4 cups vegetable broth or water
- 2 celery stalks, chopped
- 1 medium onion, chopped
- 2 carrots, chopped
- Shredded carrot, for garnish (optional)

1. In the electric pressure cooker, combine the peas, broth, celery, onion, carrots, garlic, herbes de Provence, and liquid smoke.
2. Stir the soup and season with salt and pepper.
3. Spoon into serving bowls and sprinkle shredded carrots on top (if using).

PER SERVING

Calories: 285 | Fat: 1.1g | Protein: 19.1g | Carbs: 51.9g | Fiber: 21.1g | Sugar: 9.0g | Sodium: 61mg

Pumpkin Soup

Prep time: 15 minutes | Cook time: 30 minutes | Serves 6

- 2 cups seafood broth, divided
- 1 bunch collard greens, stemmed and cut into ribbons
- 1 tomato, chopped
- 1 garlic clove, minced
- 2 (5-ounce) cans boneless, skinless salmon in water, rinsed

1. In a heavy-bottomed large stockpot, bring ½ cup of broth to a simmer over medium heat.
2. Add the salmon and cook for 3 minutes, or just enough for the flavors to come together.

PER SERVING:

Calories: 152 | Total Fat: 2g | Cholesterol: 14mg | Sodium: 213mg | Total Carbs: 19g | Sugar: 4g | Fiber: 4g | Protein: 14g

Clam Chowder

Prep time: 10 minutes | Cook time: 15 minutes | Serves 4

- 2 tablespoons extra-virgin olive oil
- 3 slices pepper bacon, chopped
- 1 onion, chopped
- 1 red bell pepper, seeded and chopped
- 1 fennel bulb, chopped
- ½ teaspoon sea salt
- ½ cup milk

1. In a large pot over medium-high heat, heat the olive oil until it shimmers. Add the bacon and cook, stirring, until browned, about 4 minutes. Remove the bacon from the fat with a slotted spoon, and set it aside on a plate.
2. Stir in the milk and return the bacon to the pot. Cook, stirring, 1 minute more.

PER SERVING

Calories: 336 | Fat: 20.1g | Protein: 20.1g | Carbs: 20.9g | Fiber: 3.1g | Sugar: 11.4g | Sodium: 495mg

Italian Vegetable Soup

Prep time: 10 minutes | Cook time: 30 minutes | Serves 5

- 8 cups vegetable broth
- 2 tablespoons olive oil
- 1 tablespoon Italian seasoning
- 1 onion, large and diced
- 2 bay leaves, dried
- 4 garlic cloves, minced
- 28 oz. tomatoes, diced

1. Set a Dutch oven with oil over medium heat.
2. Once the oil becomes hot, stir in the onions and pepper; cook for almost 10 minutes or until the onion is softened and browned.
3. Mix until everything comes together. Bring the mixture to a boil. Serve hot.

PER SERVING

Calories: 79; Fat 2g | Total Carbs: 8g | Net Carbs: 2g | Protein: 2g | Sugar: 1g | Fiber: 2g

Creamy Sweet Potato Soup

Prep time: 15 minutes | Cook time: 10 minutes | Serves 6

- 2 tablespoons avocado oil
- 1 small onion, chopped
- 2 celery stalks, chopped
- 2 teaspoons minced garlic
- 1 teaspoon kosher salt

1. Set the electric pressure cooker to the Sauté setting. When the pot is hot, pour in the avocado oil.
2. Sauté the onion and celery for 3 to 5 minutes or until the vegetables begin to soften.
3. Spoon into bowls and serve topped with Greek yogurt, parsley, and/or pumpkin seeds (if using).

PER SERVING

Calories: 193 | Total Fat: 5g | Protein: 3g | Carbs: 36g | Sugars: 8g | Fiber: 6g | Sodium: 302mg

Lentil Vegetable Soup

Prep time: 10 minutes | Cook time: 15 minutes | Serves 4

- 2 tablespoons extra-virgin olive oil
- 1 onion, finely chopped
- 1 carrot, chopped
- 1 cup chopped kale (stems removed)
- 3 garlic cloves, minced
- ¼ teaspoon freshly ground black pepper

1. In a large pot over medium-high heat, heat the olive oil until it shimmers. Add the garlic and cook, stirring constantly, for 30 seconds.
2. Stir in the lentils, vegetable broth, rosemary, salt, and pepper. Bring to a simmer. Simmer, stirring occasionally, for 5 minutes more.

PER SERVING

Calories: 160 | Total Fat: 7g | Saturated Fat: 1g | Sodium: 187mg | Carbs: 19g | Fiber: 6g | Protein: 6g

Asian Meatball Soup

Prep time: 15 minutes | Cook time: 5 hours | Serves 4

- ½ pound (227 g) ground pork
- 4 cup mustard greens, torn
- 4 scallions, sliced thin
- ¾ teaspoon red pepper flakes,
- ½ teaspoon cumin seeds, chopped coarse
- Sea salt and black pepper, to taste

1. In a large bowl, combine pork, garlic, ginger, and spices. Use your hands to combine all thoroughly.
2. Heat oil in a large skillet over medium heat. Use a slotted spoon to transfer the meatballs to a crock pot.
3. Add remaining and stir. Cover and cook on low for 4 to 5 hours or until meatballs are cooked through. Serve.

PER SERVING

Calories: 157 | Fat: 6.0g | Protein: 19.0g | Carbs: 7.1g | Fiber: 2.0g | Sugar: 2.1g | Sodium: 571mg

Black Beans Chicken Stew

Prep time: 10 minutes | Cook time: 30 minutes | Serves 4

- 1 tablespoon vegetable oil
- 1 (10 oz.) can tomatoes with chile peppers, diced
- 1 (15 oz.) can black beans, rinsed
- 1 (8.75 oz.) can kernel corn, drained
- 1 pinch ground cumin

1. In a suitable skillet, heat oil over medium-high heat.
2. Brown chicken breasts on both sides.
3. Add tomatoes with green chile peppers, beans and corn.
4. Reduce heat and let simmer for almost 25 to 30 minutes or until chicken is cooked through and juices run clear.
5. Add a dash of cumin and serve.

PER SERVING

Calories: 310; Fat 6g | Total Carbs: 28g | Net Carbs: 2g | Protein: 35g | Fiber: 3g | Sugars: 6g

Chapter 9

Grains, Legumes, and Pasta Assortments

Barley Squash Risotto

Prep time: 10 minutes | Cook time: 15 minutes | Serves 6

- 1 teaspoon extra-virgin olive oil
- ½ sweet onion, finely chopped
- 1 teaspoon minced garlic
- 2 cups cooked barley
- 2 cups chopped kale
- 2 tablespoons chopped pistachios
- 1 tablespoon chopped fresh thyme
- sea salt

1. Place a large skillet over medium heat and add the oil.
2. Sauté the onion and garlic until softened and translucent, about 3 minutes.
3. Cook until the dish is hot, about 4 minutes, and season with salt.

PER SERVING

Calories: 159 | Total Fat: 2g | Cholesterol: 0mg | Sodium: 62mg | Total Carbs: 32g | Sugar: 2g | Fiber: 7g | Protein: 5g

Light Beer Bread

Prep time: 5 minutes| Cook time: 55 minutes| Serves 14

- ¼ cup butter, soft
- 12 oz. light beer
- 3 cup low carb baking mix
- 1/3 cup Splenda

1. Heat oven to 375 degrees. Use 1 tablespoon butter to grease the bottom of a 9x5-inch loaf pan.
2. In a large bowl, whisk together beer, baking mix, and Splenda. Pour into prepared pan.
3. Bake 45-55 minutes or until golden from pan and cool on wire rack.
4. In a small glass bowl, melt remaining butter in a microwave and brush over warm loaf. Cool 15 minutes before slicing.

PER SERVING

Calories: 162 |Total Carbs: 16g |Net Carbs: 12g |Protein: 9g |Fat: 5g |Sugar: 5g |Fiber: 4g

Rainbow Black Bean Salad

Prep time: 15 minutes | Cook time: 15 minutes | Serves 5

- 1 (15-ounce) can low-sodium black beans, drained and rinsed
- 1 avocado, diced
- ¼ cup chopped fresh cilantro
- 2 tablespoons freshly squeezed lime juice
- 1 tablespoon extra-virgin olive oil
- 2 garlic cloves, minced
- 1 teaspoon honey
- ¼ teaspoon salt
- ¼ teaspoon freshly ground black pepper

1. In a large bowl, combine the black beans, avocado, tomatoes, spinach, bell pepper, jicama, scallions, and cilantro.
2. Chill for 1 hour before serving.

PER SERVING

Calories: 169 | Total Fat: 7g | Protein: 6g | Carbs: 22g | Sugars: 3g | Fiber: 9g | Sodium: 235mg

Pasta with Sweet and Spicy Seafood

Prep time: 10 minutes | Cook time: 10 minutes | Serves 4

- ¼ lb. shrimp, peel & devein
- ¼ lb. scallops
- ¼ cup extra virgin olive oil
- 3 cloves garlic, diced fine
- 1½ tbsp. salt
- ¾ tsp. red pepper flakes
- ½ recipe Homemade Pasta,

1. In a big pot, heat the oil over high heat.
2. Cook, stirring regularly, until the onion is tender, about 1 minute.
3. Cook for another minute, stirring occasionally.
4. Serve right away.

PER SERVING

Calories: 334 | Total Carbs: 13g | Net Carbs: 11g | Protein: 25g | Fat: 21g | Sugar: 6g | Fiber: 2g

Easy Coconut Quinoa

Prep time: 15 minutes | Cook time: 25 minutes | Serves 4

- 2 teaspoons extra-virgin olive oil
- 1 sweet onion, chopped
- 1 tablespoon grated fresh ginger
- 2 teaspoons minced garlic
- 1 cup low-sodium chicken broth
- 1 cup coconut milk
- Sea salt, to taste
- ¼ cup shredded, unsweetened coconut

1. Place a large saucepan over medium-high heat and add the oil.
2. Sauté the onion, ginger, and garlic until softened, about 3 minutes.
3. Add the chicken broth, coconut milk, and quinoa.
4. Season the quinoa with salt, and serve topped with the coconut.

PER SERVING

Calories: 355 | Fat: 21.1g | Protein: 9.1g | Carbs: 35.1g | Fiber: 6.1g | Sugar: 4.0g | Sodium: 33mg

Tomato and Navy Bean Bake

Prep time: 10 minutes | Cook time: 25 minutes | Serves 8

- 1 teaspoon extra-virgin olive oil
- ½ sweet onion, chopped
- 2 teaspoons minced garlic
- 2 sweet potatoes, peeled and diced
- ¼ cup sodium-free tomato paste
- 2 tablespoons granulated sweetener
- 2 tablespoons hot sauce
- 1 tablespoon Dijon mustard
- 1 tablespoon chopped fresh oregano

1. Place a large saucepan over medium-high heat and add the oil.
2. Reduce the heat and simmer the tomato sauce for 10 minutes.
3. Stir in the beans and simmer for 10 minutes more.
4. Stir in the oregano and serve.

PER SERVING

Calories: 256 | Fat: 2.1g | Protein: 15.1g | Carbs: 48.1g | Fiber: 11.9g | Sugar: 8.1g | Sodium: 150mg

Green Beans and Crispy Baked Flounder

Prep time: 10 minutes | Cook time: 20 minutes | serves 4

- 1 lb. flounder
- 2 cups green beans
- 4 tbsp. plant-based butter
- 8 basil leaves
- What you'll need from store cupboard:
- 3 cloves garlic
- Salt and pepper to taste
- Nonstick cooking spray

1. Preheat the oven to 350 °Fahrenheit.
2. Using cooking spray, coat a baking dish.
3. Place the butter on top, cut into small pieces.
4. Bake for 15-20 minutes, or until the fish readily flakes with a fork.
5. Serve.

PER SERVING

Calories: 358 | Total Carbs: 5g | Net Carbs: 2g | Protein: 39.0g | Fat: 8.0g | Sugar: 1g | Fiber: 2 g

Butter Beans

Prep time: 15 minutes | Cook time: 15 minutes | Serves 6

- ½ cup Vegetable Broth or store-bought low-sodium vegetable broth
- 2 celery stalks, thinly sliced
- ½ Vidalia onion, thinly sliced
- 1 garlic clove, minced
- 2 (15-ounce) cans low-sodium butter beans
- ¼ teaspoon Not Old Bay Seasoning

1. In a medium skillet, bring the broth to a simmer over medium heat.
2. Add the celery, onion, and garlic and cook for 3 to 5 minutes, or until they soften.
3. Add the beans and seasoning, cover, and continue to cook for 5 to 7 minutes, or until the flavors come together.
4. Enjoy with Spicy Mustard Greens.

PER SERVING:

Calories: 126 | Total Fat: 1g | Cholesterol: 0mg | Sodium: 112mg | Total Carbs: 21g | Sugar: 1g | Fiber: 5g | Protein: 7g

Chapter 10

Heavenly Snacks and Sweets

Apple Crunch

Prep time: 13 minutes | Cook time: 2 minutes | Serves 4

- 3 apples, peeled, cored, and sliced (about 1½ pounds)
- 1 teaspoon pure maple syrup
- ¼ cup low-sugar granola

1. In the electric pressure cooker, combine the apples, maple syrup, apple pie spice, and apple juice.
2. Close and lock the lid of the pressure cooker. Set the valve to sealing.
3. Spoon the apples into 4 serving bowls and sprinkle each with 1 tablespoon of granola.

PER SERVING

Calories: 103 | Total Fat: 1g | Protein: 1g | Carbs: 26g | Sugars: 18g | Fiber: 4g | Sodium: 13mg

German Chocolate Cake Bars

Prep time: 10 minutes| Cook time: 5 minutes| Serves 20

- 2 cup unsweetened coconut flakes
- 1 cup coconut milk, divided
- ¾ cup chopped pecans
- nonstick cooking spray

1. Spray an 8x8-inch baking dish with cooking spray.
2. In a large bowl, combine the coconut, and pecan, stir to combine.
3. Pour chocolate over the coconut layer and chill 1 hour, or until set. Cut into squares to serve.

PER SERVING

Calories: 245 |Total Carbs: 12g |Net Carbs: 9g |Protein: 3g |Fat: 19g |Sugar: 7g |Fiber: 3g

Chai Pear-Fig Compote

Prep time: 20 minutes | **Cook time:** 3 minutes |
Serves 4

- 1 vanilla chai tea bag
- 1 (3-inch) cinnamon stick
- ½ cup chopped dried figs
- 2 tablespoons raisins

1. Pour 1 cup of water into the electric pressure cooker and hit Sauté/More. Let the tea steep for 5 minutes, then remove and discard the tea bag.
2. Close and lock the lid of the pressure cooker. Set the valve to sealing.

PER SERVING

Calories: 167 | Total Fat: 1g | Protein: 2g | Carbs: 44g | Sugars: 29g | Fiber: 9g | Sodium: 4mg

Avocado Chocolate Mousse

Prep time: 5 minutes | **Cook time:** 5 minutes |
Serves 4

- 2 avocados, mashed
- ¼ cup canned coconut milk
- 2 tablespoons unsweetened cocoa powder
- 2 tablespoons pure maple syrup
- ½ teaspoon espresso powder

1. In a blender, combine all of the ingredients. Blend until smooth.
2. Pour the mixture into 4 small bowls and serve.

PER SERVING

Calories: 203 | Total Fat: 17g | Saturated Fat: 7g | Sodium: 11mg | Carbs: 15g | Fiber: 6g | Protein: 2g

Cheesy Onion Dip

Prep time: 5 minutes| Cook time: 5 minutes| Serves 8

- 8 oz. low fat cream cheese, soft
- 1 cup onions, grated
- 1 cup low fat Swiss cheese, grated
- 1 cup lite mayonnaise

1. Heat oven to broil.
2. Combine all ingredients in a small casserole dish. Microwave on high, stirring every 30 seconds, until cheese is melted and ingredients are combined.
3. Place under the broiler for 1-2 minutes until the top is nicely browned. Serve warm with vegetables for dipping.

PER SERVING

Calories: 158 |Total Carbs: 5g |Protein: 9g |Fat: 11g |Sugar: 1g |Fiber: 0g

Oatmeal Cookies

Prep time: 5 minutes | Cook time: 15 minutes | Serves 16 (1 cookie each)

- ¾ cup almond flour
- ¾ cup old-fashioned oats
- ¼ cup shredded unsweetened coconut
- 1 teaspoon baking powder
- 1 teaspoon ground cinnamon
- ¼ teaspoon salt
- ¼ cup unsweetened applesauce
- 1 large egg
- 1 tablespoon pure maple syrup
- 2 tablespoons coconut oil, melted

1. Preheat the oven to 350°F.
2. Using a spatula, remove the cookies and cool on a rack.

PER SERVING

Calories: 76 | Total Fat: 6g | Protein: 2g | Carbs: 5g | Sugars: 1g | Fiber: 1g | Sodium: 57mg

Jewel Yams with Nutmeg

Prep time: 7 minutes | Cook time: 45 minutes | Serves 8

- 2 medium jewel yams
- 2 tablespoons unsalted butter
- Juice of 1 large orange
- 1½ teaspoons ground cinnamon
- ¼ teaspoon ground ginger
- ¾ teaspoon ground nutmeg
- ⅛ teaspoon ground cloves

1. Set the oven at 355 °F.
2. Arrange the yam dices on a rimmed baking sheet in a single layer.
3. Set aside.
4. Bake in the preheated oven for 40 minutes.
5. Let the yams cool for 8 minutes on the baking sheet before removing and serving.

PER SERVING

Calories: 129 | Total Carbs: 10g | Net Carbs: 6g | Protein: 11g | Fat: 9g | Sugars 1 g | Fiber: 3g

Peach, Banana, and Almond Pancakes

Prep time: 15 minutes | Cook time: 15 minutes | Serves 7

- 2 cups peaches, chopped
- 4 ripe bananas, peeled
- 2 medium egg whites
- 1 medium egg
- ¼ teaspoon almond extract
- ¾ cup almond meal

1. Preheat the oven to 400°F (205°C).
2. Put all the ingredients in a food processor, and pulse until mix well and it has a thick consistency.
3. Pour the mixture in a baking dish lined with parchment paper.
4. Remove the pancakes from the oven and slice to serve.

PER SERVING

Calories: 166 | Fat: 6.9g | Protein: 6.1g | Carbs: 21.8g | Fiber: 4.2g | sugars: 11.8g | Sodium: 22mg

Grilled Sesame Tofu

Prep time: 45 minutes | Cook time: 10 minutes |
Serves 6

- 1½ tablespoons brown rice vinegar
- 1 scallion
- 2 tablespoons naturally brewed soy sauce
- ¼ teaspoon dried red pepper flakes
- 2 tablespoons cilantro
- 1 teaspoon sesame seeds

1. Combine the vinegar, scallion, ginger, applesauce, soy sauce, red pepper flakes, and sesame oil in a suitable bowl.
2. Stir to mix well.
3. Preheat a grill pan over medium-high heat.
4. Serve with the marinade alongside.

PER SERVING

Calories: 189 | Total Carbs: 7.9g | Net Carbs: 4.5g | Protein: 6g | Fat: 10g | Sugars 1 g | Fiber: 5g

Tex Mex Popcorn

Prep time: 5 minutes| Cook time: 5 minutes|
Serves 4

- ¼ cup cilantro, diced
- refrigerated butter-flavor spray
- 4 cup popcorn
- 1 tsp chili powder
- ½ tsp salt
- ½ tsp cumin seeds
- ½ tsp garlic powder
- 1/8 tsp smoked paprika

1. Place popcorn in a large bowl and spritz with butter spray. Add remaining ingredients and toss to coat. Continue spritzing and tossing until popcorn is well coated.
2. Store in an airtight container. Serving size is 1 cup.

PER SERVING

Calories: 32 |Total Carbs: 6g |Net Carbs: 5g |Protein: 1g |Fat: 0g |Sugar: 0g |Fiber: 1g

Appendix 1 Measurement Conversion Chart

Volume Equivalents (Dry)	
US STANDARD	**METRIC (APPROXIMATE)**
1/8 teaspoon	0.5 mL
1/4 teaspoon	1 mL
1/2 teaspoon	2 mL
3/4 teaspoon	4 mL
1 teaspoon	5 mL
1 tablespoon	15 mL
1/4 cup	59 mL
1/2 cup	118 mL
3/4 cup	177 mL
1 cup	235 mL
2 cups	475 mL
3 cups	700 mL
4 cups	1 L

Volume Equivalents (Liquid)		
US STANDARD	**US STANDARD (OUNCES)**	**METRIC (AP-PROXIMATE)**
2 tablespoons	1 fl.oz.	30 mL
1/4 cup	2 fl.oz.	60 mL
1/2 cup	4 fl.oz.	120 mL
1 cup	8 fl.oz.	240 mL
1 1/2 cup	12 fl.oz.	355 mL
2 cups or 1 pint	16 fl.oz.	475 mL
4 cups or 1 quart	32 fl.oz.	1 L
1 gallon	128 fl.oz.	4 L

Temperatures Equivalents	
FAHRENHEIT(F)	**CELSIUS(C) APPROXIMATE)**
225 °F	107 °C
250 °F	120 ° °C
275 °F	135 °C
300 °F	150 °C
325 °F	160 °C
350 °F	180 °C
375 °F	190 °C
400 °F	205 °C
425 °F	220 °C
450 °F	235 °C
475 °F	245 °C
500 °F	260 °C

Weight Equivalents	
US STANDARD	**METRIC (APPROXIMATE)**
1 ounce	28 g
2 ounces	57 g
5 ounces	142 g
10 ounces	284 g
15 ounces	425 g
16 ounces (1 pound)	455 g
1.5 pounds	680 g
2 pounds	907 g

Appendix 2 The Dirty Dozen and Clean Fifteen

The Environmental Working Group (EWG) is a nonprofit, nonpartisan organization dedicated to protecting human health and the environment Its mission is to empower people to live healthier lives in a healthier environment. This organization publishes an annual list of the twelve kinds of produce, in sequence, that have the highest amount of pesticide residue-the Dirty Dozen-as well as a list of the fifteen kinds ofproduce that have the least amount of pesticide residue-the Clean Fifteen.

THE DIRTY DOZEN

The 2016 Dirty Dozen includes the following produce. These are considered among the year's most important produce to buy organic:

Strawberries	Spinach
Apples	Tomatoes
Nectarines	Bell peppers
Peaches	Cherry tomatoes
Celery	Cucumbers
Grapes	Kale/collard greens
Cherries	Hot peppers

The Dirty Dozen list contains two additional itemskale/collard greens and hot peppers-because they tend to contain trace levels of highly hazardous pesticides.

THE CLEAN FIFTEEN

The least critical to buy organically are the Clean Fifteen list. The following are on the 2016 list:

Avocados	Papayas
Corn	Kiw
Pineapples	Eggplant
Cabbage	Honeydew
Sweet peas	Grapefruit
Onions	Cantaloupe
Asparagus	Cauliflower
Mangos	

Some of the sweet corn sold in the United States are made from genetically engineered (GE) seedstock. Buy organic varieties of these crops to avoid GE produce.

Appendix 3 Index

Karly T. Whittington

Printed in Great Britain
by Amazon